Active Reader's Practice Book

PROGRAM DESIGNER AND GENERAL EDITOR
Kylene Beers, Ed.D.
UNIVERSITY OF HOUSTON

ELEMENTS OF
Literature
INTRODUCTORY
COURSE

Jairo Jimene

MiniReads
MiniRead Practice Activity Worksheets
Selection Practice Activity Worksheets
Additional Practice Graphic Organizers

HOLT, RINEHART AND WINSTON
Harcourt Brace & Company
Austin • New York • Orlando • Atlanta • San Francisco • Boston • Dallas • Toronto • London

Staff Credits

Director: Mescal Evler

Manager of Editorial Operations: Bill Wahlgren

Managing Editor: Marie Price

Executive Editor: Patricia A. McCambridge

Project Editor: Victoria Moreland

Component Editors: Pamela Thompson, Scott Hall, Tracy DeMont

Editorial Staff: *Assistant Editor,* Chi Nguyen; *Copyediting Manager,* Michael Neibergall; *Senior Copyeditor,* Mary Malone; *Copyeditors,* Joel Bourgeois, Gabrielle Field, Suzi A. Hunn, Jane Kominek, Millicent Ondras, Theresa Reding, Désirée Reid, Kathleen Scheiner; *Editorial Coordinators,* Marcus Johnson, Mark Holland, Jill O'Neal, Janet Riley; *Support Staff,* Lori De La Garza; *Word Processors,* Ruth Hooker, Margaret Sanchez, Gail Coupland

Research and Development: Joan Burditt

Permissions: Tamara A. Blanken, Ann B. Farrar

Design: *Art Director, Book & Media Design,* Joe Melomo

Prepress Production: Beth Prevelige, Simira Davis, Sergio Durante

Media Production: *Production Manager,* Kim A. Scott; *Production Coordinator,* Belinda Barbosa; *Production Supervisor,* Nancy Hargis

Manufacturing Coordinator: Michael Roche

Printed in the United States of America

ISBN 0-03-064574-3

234567 22 02 01

To the Student

This *Reading Skills and Strategies: Active Reader's Practice Book* is a resource for you, the student, to use in conjunction with your teacher's *Reading Skills and Strategies* binder. In this booklet, you will find materials made specifically for you: texts and activity worksheets that you can write on, draw on, and mark up in any way that helps you to become a more active, involved reader.

This *Reading Skills and Strategies: Active Reader's Practice Book* is designed to be used with your *Elements of Literature* anthology. In this book, you will find four different kinds of reading materials and practice activities that will help you to become a more confident user of reading strategies: MiniReads, MiniRead Practice Activity Worksheets, Selection Practice Activity Worksheets, and Additional Practice graphic organizers (for use with particular reading strategies).

MiniReads are short, high-interest reading selections that will help you to develop and practice specific reading skills and strategies. In the margins of every MiniRead, there is ample room for you to write your own notes and comments as you read. You can also mark the MiniReads in any way that you find helpful, highlighting important passages or circling words and phrases that seem especially significant. Each MiniRead is followed by a **MiniRead Practice Activity Worksheet** that gives you an opportunity to apply the skills and strategies you have learned in that particular MiniRead lesson. Many of the activities on these worksheets involve group or partner work, but you or your teacher can adjust and customize the lessons in any ways that you wish.

In addition to the MiniReads and their accompanying MiniRead Practice Activity Worksheets, you will also find **Selection Practice Activity Worksheets**. These worksheets accompany specific selections in your *Elements of Literature* anthology, giving you opportunities to apply the reading skills and strategies you have learned through the MiniRead to specific selections in your textbook. The reading skill presented in a Selection Practice Activity Worksheet will be the same Reading Skills and Strategies (RSS) skill that appears on the selection's Before You Read page in your Pupil's Edition. Selection Practice Activity Worksheets include a variety of interesting, interactive tasks that will help you build reading skills and strategies that you can transfer to any kind of reading that you do, whether it be reading your school textbooks, enjoying an entertaining novel, or reading a magazine for information.

Finally, at the back of this book, in a section called Additional Practice, you'll find graphic organizers that you can use to help you with various reading strategies that you may find yourself using again and again, such as Somebody Wanted But So, It Says . . . I Say, and Think-Aloud, among others. You will find it helpful to use these graphic organizers in a variety of reading situations, both inside and outside of class.

Active readers interact with texts in a variety of ways. This booklet provides you with opportunities to take notes, mark up texts, and complete reading skills and strategies activities that will build your reading skills and help to make you a more confident, engaged reader.

ABOUT THE MINIREAD WRITERS

Joan Burditt has a Master's Degree in Education with a specialization in reading. She has taught in regular classrooms as well as in programs for struggling readers. Currently a program development consultant, she has written for educational publishers and magazines on a wide range of subjects.

Richard Cohen is an educational writer and editor as well as a novelist. He has written a college creative-writing textbook, *Writer's Mind: Crafting Fiction*, and the novels *Domestic Tranquillity, Don't Mention the Moon,* and *Say You Want Me.* A graduate of the University of Michigan, he has taught creative writing at the University of Wisconsin, Madison.

Ed Combs is a freelance writer and editor. Combs graduated from St. Edward's University in Austin, Texas, and has written and edited for educational publishers, standardized testing companies, magazines, and newspapers for fifteen years. He taught English and basketball to at-risk students in Atlanta, Georgia.

Tom Dowe graduated from Yale College and received an M.A. in English and American Literature from The University of Texas at Austin. He has written for *Wired, Mother Jones, The New York Times Magazine,* and many web-based magazines. His poetry and prose have appeared in numerous literary journals. He is currently writing a biography of the poet Kenneth Koch.

Tracy Duncan is an artist, writer, and editor. She graduated from The University of Texas at Austin and has written and edited for textbook publishers, standardized testing companies, magazines, and newspapers for fourteen years. She served as an Artist-in-Residence for the Atlanta Project.

Corinne Greiner is a freelance writer. She attended the Iowa Writers' Workshop and the Radcliffe Publishing Institute on fellowships. A winner of the Bank of America Award for Young Writers, she was also a finalist for the Annie Dillard Award in Nonfiction and a nominee for the Pushcart Prize.

Patty Kolar taught secondary English, journalism, and reading for ten years. A Phi Beta Kappa graduate of The University of Texas at Austin, she was curriculum coordinator for an after-school child-care agency and currently works in the research and curriculum department of a leading educational publisher.

Mary Beth Mader has worked as an advertising copywriter and is currently a philosophy instructor. She holds a Ph.D. in Philosophy. She was a 1992 recipient of the French government's Chateaubriand Fellowship and is the translator of Luce Irigaray's *The Forgetting of Air in Martin Heidegger.*

Mimi Mayer received an M.F.A. in Creative Writing from the University of Michigan, where she lectured in composition and rhetoric from 1990–1993. Her work has been recognized with twelve national and regional awards from such organizations as the Council for the Advancement and Support of Education, the International Association of Business Communicators, and the Michigan Press Association. A published poet, Mayer has received fellowships from the Cranbook and the Aspen Writing Foundations.

Mary Olmstead, formerly a middle and high school English and French teacher, currently writes and edits for textbook publishing and testing companies. Past awards include National Endowment for the Humanities grants to study the teaching of literature, and grants from the French government and the U.S. Department of Defense for travel to France and the French Antilles to study the French culture.

Carrie Laing Pickett is a freelance writer, editor, and poet who writes and edits for educational publishers. She holds an M.F.A. in Poetry.

Mara Rockliff is a freelance writer and editor with a degree in American Civilization from Brown University. Currently residing in Louisa, Virginia, she has written several adaptations and other works for leading literature textbooks, as well as plays in a book titled *Plays for Classroom Performance*.

Nancy Shreve graduated from Kent State University in 1987 with a B.A. in English and Education. She has interned for Kent State University Press, taught middle school for six years, and is currently pursuing a degree in creative writing.

Adrienne Su studied at Harvard and the University of Virginia. She has had fellowships at Yaddo in Saratoga Springs, New York; the MacDowell Colony in Petersborough, New Hampshire; and the Fine Arts Work Center in Provincetown, Massachusetts. A former member of New York City's national poetry-slam team, she writes about contemporary poetry for the Scholastic magazine *Literary Cavalcade* and is the author of a book of poems, *Middle Kingdom* (1997).

Jeanne Claire van Ryzin received a B.A. in English from Columbia University and an M.A. in Creative Writing from The University of Texas at Austin. She has been a writing resident at the Ragdale Foundation in Lake Forest, Illinois. Her fiction has received a PEN Syndicated Fiction award, and she has been a finalist for the Hemingway Short Story Award and the Nelson Algren Award. She has written articles for *The New York Times* and other newspapers.

Lisa Weckerle received an M.A. in Performance Studies from The University of North Carolina at Chapel Hill and is currently pursuing a Ph.D. in Performance Studies. She has written for the *Berkeley Fiction Review* and the *New Writer's Showcase*. She has taught classes for both children and adults in children's theater, playwriting, and dramatic performance, and has directed over twenty-five plays for varied audiences.

Sarah Wolbach is a poet, educational writer, and editor. She received her M.F.A. in Poetry from the Texas Center for Writers at The University of Texas at Austin in 1996. The recipient of a post-graduate fellowship, she spent the 1996–1997 academic year in San Miguel de Allende, Mexico.

The Winter Catcher (FICTION) (page 1)

Baseball practice is difficult when you're trying to pitch alone in drifts of snow. This story and its companion piece **"Just Once"** (Pupil's Edition, page 2) prove that sports aren't always as simple as they look.

The Day for Growing Up (FICTION) (page 7)

How do different cultures celebrate hallmarks in a child's life? This piece takes us through the events of one girl's quinceañera, or fifteenth birthday party, and one boy's high school graduation day. It is a companion piece for **"Ta-Na-E-Ka"** (Pupil's Edition, page 15), which shows us yet another rite of passage. Though the practices vary, all cultures have some form of ritual for the difficult job of growing up.

Basketball Pivot (FICTION) (page 13)

The basketball court is home to Mary Ruth, who seems as if she were born with a basketball in her hands. She's tall and talented. She's also the target of one student's ridicule. This story is paired with **"The All-American Slurp"** (Pupil's Edition, page 31), and both stories serve as reminders that our differences make us interesting.

The Playoff (FICTION) (page 21)

On the one hand, being the center of attention is exciting, whether it's on stage or on a volleyball court. On the other hand, it can be excruciating, especially if your performance is less than perfect. The character in this MiniRead has something in common with Manuel in **"La Bamba"** (Pupil's Edition, page 44). So do you, if you've ever been embarrassed in front of a crowd.

Beanie Baby™ Madness (NONFICTION) (page 29)

Maybe the madness has worn off, but the lesson in economics hasn't. This piece explores the law of supply and demand as well as the art of collecting. The article about a popular toy is a companion piece for the selection **"President Cleveland, Where Are You?"** (Pupil's Edition, page 53). What will Jerry have to do to get one more trading card?

A Ledge to Grind On (FICTION) (page 35)

Three boys have found the perfect place to perform stunts on their skateboards—in front of a lonely woman's house. They think she's bitter and angry. Their feelings change after one of them injures himself. They learn that first impressions are often wrong, just as the main character does in the selection **"The Stone"** (Pupil's Edition, page 69).

Brothers Forever (NONFICTION) (page 43)

Vincent and Theo Van Gogh were about as close as two brothers can get, even though their relationship was stormy at times. This MiniRead about their relationship is paired with **"Brother"** (Pupil's Edition, page 109), in which Maya Angelou tells us about her love for her brother, Bailey.

The *Amistad* Chronicles (NONFICTION) (page 49)

In 1839, a group of Africans was kidnapped and carried across the ocean to Cuba. This MiniRead tells the story of their survival and eventual liberation. It is a companion piece for **"A Glory over Everything"** (Pupil's Edition, page 136), a selection that tells the story of Harriet Tubman, a slave who fought unrelentingly for freedom.

The Fairy Godmother Failure (PLAY) (page 71)

What if your Fairy Godmother only made your life worse? This play is a modern-day twist on a classic fairy tale. It is a companion piece for ***The Adventure of the Speckled Band*** (Pupil's Edition, page 408), one of three plays that appear in this unit.

Why the Bat Flies at Night (FOLK TALE) (page 83)

The bat wasn't always dark and furry. According to folklore, it once looked like a beautiful bird—until its trickery was discovered. This story is a companion to **"The Seventh Sister"** (Pupil's Edition, page 528), another how-and-why tale.

Welcome Your Guests with Hospitality (NONFICTION) (page 95)

In **"Baucis and Philemon"** (Pupil's Edition, page 589), the title characters make a good decision when they welcome Zeus and Hermes into their home. They exhibit all the traits of good Greek hosts. How do other cultures show hospitality? This MiniRead presents readers with information about hospitality around the world.

MiniReads, MiniRead Practice Activity Worksheets, and Selection Practice Activity Worksheets

The Winter Catcher

1   The sky outside was white with snow, and all Raquel could think about was baseball. She rolled over on her bed to look at the Orioles calendar hanging above her desk. She knew it would be three months until the spring youth league started up, but she wanted to see the little blocks of numbers, the months of days all lined up, to get a good picture of exactly how many baseball-less days she would have to wait. A lot, that's how many.

2   *Thwock.* She could almost hear the sweet sound of the ball's impact: not too hard, not too soft, fitting the glove just right. Raquel wanted to play ball, and she wanted to play now.

3   She threw on her boots and jacket and baseball cap, hoping this would count as being "bundled up" to any grown-up who saw her as she left the house. Her uncle spotted her at the back door. "Bundle up more," he ordered. She put on her red wool snow hat and pulled the baseball cap on top. "That sure looks dumb," she decided, and tossed the baseball cap onto a curving hook of the coat stand on her way to the door. "Hey, what about gloves?" her uncle asked. Raquel grabbed her baseball glove, put it on, and then had a hard time turning the door handle. "I've got my glove!" she called back to him and jumped down the stone steps into the cold.

4   "I don't have what I really need," she thought. "I don't have a catcher. What good is a pitcher without a catcher?" She had had this problem already this week, when none of her friends in the neighborhood could or would play ball with her. Carolyn, her regular catcher, had moved away. Justin was sick and hadn't been out of his pajamas for days. All Velma wanted to do was go sledding on the new snow and skating on the ice. Marcus's fingers got too cold to throw the ball, and so on. "I guess baseball is a spring and summer sport," she thought, "but I don't see why." She took off her glove, scooped up some fresh snow, and formed it into a

ELEMENTS OF LITERATURE

beautiful round ball. She noticed that the fence posts wore their own kind of snow hats. She took aim at one of them. The flying snowball swept the snow cleanly off the top of the post. Her red fingers were forming a second snowball when she had an idea. She took her snowball and began to roll it across the snow-covered ground, stopping only to pack on the snow that the ball picked up. Raquel then built the standard three-ball snowman, piling a medium-sized ball on a big ball, and a small ball on the medium-sized one. She was getting so warm pushing these snowballs around the yard that she took off her wool hat and stuck it on the snowman's head.

5   She stood back. "Almost," she thought, and she punched the snowman in the stomach. "Sorry about that," she said, her arm deep in the thick snow belly. She yanked her arm out, went around behind the snowman, and pushed and dug through the snowy back. Then she squatted and looked through—yep, she'd made a hole all the way through. Raquel reached into the hole, making it bigger and smoothing its sides. "I think this is going to work," she thought, brushing off her ice-coated sleeve as she walked away from the strange-looking snowman.

6   At pitching distance from the snowman, she stopped and made a small pyramid of snowballs. Five per batter, fifteen per inning is what she would shoot for. She picked up the first ball from the top of the pyramid. Raquel went into her windup, raising her hands over her head, kicking her knee up high in front—and then let her no-miss fastball go. The fastball went right through the snowman's belly tunnel.

7   Raquel spent all afternoon sending balls at the snowman. Sometimes they disappeared into the hole; sometimes they broke apart in a cloud of white on the snowman, but she got better and better at sending them right through the hole. Spring was looking closer all the time.

The Winter Catcher

SKILL MONITORING COMPREHENSION | **STRATEGY** THINK-ALOUD

Directions: Work with a partner to read the MiniRead "The Winter Catcher" and make Think-Aloud comments. One partner should be the reader who reads aloud through to the end of paragraph 4, pausing to make comments, while the listener uses a tally mark to identify those comments in the *Tally* column below. Then, switch roles and continue reading and commenting to the end of the MiniRead.

Think-Aloud Tally Sheet

Listener:_____

Think-Aloud Comments	Tally
Identifying problems	
Fixing problems	
Predicting what happens next	
Picturing the text	
Making comparisons	
Making comments	

Just Once

Directions: Work with a partner to read "Just Once" (Pupil's Edition, page 2) and make Think-Aloud comments. One partner should be the reader who reads aloud Pupil's Edition pages 5–6, pausing to make comments, while the listener uses a tally mark to identify those comments in the *Tally* column below. Then, switch roles and continue to the end of the selection.

Think-Aloud Tally Sheet

Listener:_____

Think-Aloud Comments	Tally
Predicting what happens next	
Picturing the text	
Making comparisons	
Identifying problems	
Fixing problems	
Making comments	

The Day for Growing Up

1   Today is my next-door neighbor Sofie's *quinceañera*—and it also happens to be the day my brother is graduating from high school. The *quinceañera* is a large party given for Latinas on their fifteenth birthday, and so in both Sofie's house and mine there are many relatives arriving and much excitement. This morning there isn't much to do except watch Sofie and my brother working themselves up and getting elegantly dressed. So many relatives have come to town for these two celebrations, it seems like our street is having a block party.

2   At Sofie's, everyone is up early. Sofie's billowing white dress, its skirt as fat as a Christmas tree, is hanging in the living room. Sofie had wanted a pale purple dress, but her mom insisted on white, which Sofie says is really old-fashioned. Sofie is in her bathrobe. On her head is a pile of curlers, and her Aunt Luz is doing Sofie's nails. I help Sofie's brother, sister, and cousins set up chairs in the living room, on the patio, and in the yard. Then I sit next to Sofie, and she describes the *quinceañera* for me.

3   First, they will go to church for Mass, and then they will come home to get ready for the fiesta. There will be tons of food that Sofie's mom, aunts, grandmothers, and their friends have been preparing for days. There will be a band and many guests. Some kids I know from school are coming. The girls will be almost as dressed up as Sofie, and the boys will be their escorts. All of Sofie's other friends and relatives will be there, too. It will be a major event.

4   When the dance is ready to start, Sofie and her dad will be the first out on the dance floor. This part is Sofie's big moment: In her incredibly fancy off-the-shoulder dress, she will be in the spotlight. Sofie says this will be a formal ceremony presenting her as a woman to the community. At that moment, she will become an adult. I wonder if she'll think of me as a kid after that.

quinceañera:
(kēn sā ä nyā´ rä)

The Day for Growing Up (cont'd)

5   After they start the dance, every-body will join in, and the party will really begin. I plan on coming back after my brother's graduation to see what is going on and to try some of the food I have been smelling for days.

6   Back at my house, my brother Derek is in some kind of trance in front of the bathroom mirror—staring, talking to himself, and combing his hair over and over. He is supposed to give a speech at graduation, so I decide not to say anything about his bizarre behavior.

7   My uncle and aunt have gone out to buy a blank video-tape for the camera, and my mom and my grandparents are in the living room reviewing our entire lives. I head back to the bathroom and fill Derek in on what is happening at Sofie's house, but he isn't too interested at this moment. I ask Derek why high school graduation is such a big deal, and he says, "It means freedom!" I knew he would say something exaggerated and mysterious. He says that after high school, you are an adult. He says he'll be going to college and will live there instead of at home. He'll get to be on his own.

8   Derek's kind of dramatic. He's been acting like he's been living in prison for the whole last year. Mom says a semester at college will make him glad to see us when he comes home for the winter break. I'm not sure about that.

9   Suddenly everything speeds up. Mom is telling Derek to hurry up because his friends will be here soon. My aunt and uncle are back and want to see Derek in his cap and gown. My dad calls to double-check when the graduation ceremony will start. Derek can't find the shoes he wants to wear.

10   We are all out front, watching Derek talk to the video camera, when his friends show up. Derek heads for the car, waving to us as he runs away in his flapping gown, and we all go inside to get ready. Soon Derek will give his speech and get his diploma. Then, like Sophie, he will be grown-up, too.

NAME _____ | CLASS _____ | DATE _____

The Day for Growing Up

SKILL COMPARING AND CONTRASTING CULTURES | STRATEGY ANTICIPATION GUIDES

Part 1. Directions: Before reading the MiniRead "The Day for Growing Up," read the following statements and decide whether you agree or disagree with each statement. Mark an X in the appropriate blank in the *Before Reading* column. After you have read the MiniRead, mark an X in the appropriate blank in the *After Reading* column to show whether or not your views were influenced by the MiniRead. Be prepared to explain your decisions.

BEFORE READING		AFTER READING
Agree / Disagree	**Statement**	**Agree / Disagree**
___✓__ / _____	1. You cannot fully appreciate the traditions and ceremonies of a culture that isn't yours.	___✓__ / _____
_____ / ___✓__	2. The traditions and ceremonies of one culture cannot be compared with traditions and ceremonies of another culture.	_____ / ___✓__
_____ / ___✓__	3. Cultural traditions and ceremonies don't mean much anymore.	_____ / ___✓__
___✓__ / _____	4. Teenagers should take part in family traditions and ceremonies even if they don't agree with them.	___✓__ / _____

Part 2. Directions: Choose three of the Anticipation Guide statements above and, on the back of this sheet, describe how each statement you chose relates to the MiniRead.

Part 3. Directions: Think of traditions or ceremonies in your own life—informal or formal, part of your family or culture. Compare those to the traditions and ceremonies mentioned in "A Day for Growing Up." How are they alike? different?

Traditions and Ceremonies in Your Life	**How It's Like or Different from the Traditions and Ceremonies in the MiniRead**
When we have a tradition we have a birthday party	They had a party too in traditions

ELEMENTS OF LITERATURE

Active Reader's Practice Book | 9

4. Teenagers' take apart from their family
   is related to the ~~the boy~~ that is going to college
2. The tradition ceremonies is related
   to the story that they have a party.

Ta-Na-E-Ka

SKILL COMPARING AND CONTRASTING CULTURES | **STRATEGY** ANTICIPATION GUIDES

Part 1. Directions: Before reading "Ta-Na-E-Ka" (Pupil's Edition, page 15), read each of the following statements and decide whether you agree or disagree with the statement. Mark an X in the appropriate blank in the *Before Reading* column. After you have read "Ta-Na-E-Ka," mark an X in the appropriate blank in the *After Reading* column to show whether or not your views were influenced by the selection. Be prepared to explain your decisions.

BEFORE READING		AFTER READING
Agree / Disagree	Statement	Agree / Disagree
_____ / _____	1. Traditional customs should change with the times.	_____ / _____
_____ / _____	2. It is important to acknowledge the passage from one stage of life to the next.	_____ / _____
_____ / _____	3. There are right ways and wrong ways to do things.	_____ / _____
_____ / _____	4. Individuality is always more important than tradition.	_____ / _____

Part 2. Directions: Choose three of the Anticipation Guide statements above and, on the back of this sheet, describe how each statement you chose relates to the selection.

Part 3. Directions: Using the chart below, describe the similarities and differences between your culture and the culture shown in "Ta-Na-E-Ka."

Similarities	Differences

Basketball Pivot

1   Kevin Gates was the most popular kid at Carver Middle School. Every seventh-grader knew Kevin. He was smart, <u>talented</u> on the basketball court, and very funny. There was only one problem. Kevin could be mean, and no one ever tried to stop him.

2   Probably Kevin was at his worst on Mary Ruth Dunlap's first and last day at Carver. I'll never forget that day. The new girl slumped over her desk. It was as if she was trying to <u>compress</u> herself into a space she had outgrown. She also looked weird in a baggy T-shirt and jeans that weren't quite long enough.

3   The problems started when Coach Taggart, the homeroom teacher, <u>acquainted</u> the class with the new student. "This is Mary Ruth Dunlap. Her family has just moved here from Idaho. Let's welcome our new classmate," Coach Taggart said. "Please stand, Mary Ruth."

4   Once Mary Ruth stood, it was clear why she curled herself around her desk. To put it mildly, Mary Ruth was tall. Her entire body seemed to <u>consist</u> of her long, strong legs. She was almost as tall as Jason Petit, the only seventh-grader Coach Taggart allowed on Carver's varsity basketball team.

5   Then Kevin started in.

6   "Your name should be Baby Ruth," Kevin <u>jeered</u>. "Because you're teensy-weensy, like a baby."

7   "Can it, Kevin," Coach Taggart growled. Mary Ruth sank back into her chair. This behavior had almost become <u>routine</u> to her. Wherever she went, it was the same thing: people stared and children yelled, "Look at her!" She must have felt like a freak. When the bell rang, Mary Ruth ran from the room. She moved too fast to hear Coach Taggart calling her. She didn't see Coach yelling at Kevin.

8   Between classes, Kevin followed Mary Ruth down the hall, <u>intoning</u>, "Baby Ruth, Baby Ruth, teensy-weensy Baby Ruth." Mary Ruth tried to pretend she didn't hear him, but Kevin's <u>taunts</u> upset her. When she reached her locker, she discovered that someone had

taped a picture of a baby to the door. Long legs had been drawn on the baby, which made its head so tiny, so <u>minuscule</u>, that you could barely see it on top of those legs.

9   Before long, the whole school was talking about Kevin and Mary Ruth. Then Coach Taggart called a boy-girl gym class. He did this <u>occasionally</u>, but not often. It was a good chance to get extra practice.

10   Except for Mary Ruth and Kevin, Coach teamed up boys and girls for basketball drills. Kids played at six <u>temporary</u> baskets on the sidelines and at one of the <u>permanent</u> baskets used in varsity games. Teams worked on passing, dribbling, and guarding. They also worked on <u>offensive</u> plays because they were already so good at <u>defense</u>.

11   Coach turned to Mary Ruth and Kevin. "You two, go to that last hoop."

12   Kevin <u>strutted</u> toward the basket as if he were a basketball star. Halfway there, he <u>lobbed</u> the ball at Mary Ruth. She caught it easily.

13   Coach Taggart smiled. "Around the World is a good game for two players. It will show me if you can shoot," he said.

14   Coach pointed out five spots in a half-circle around the basket.

15   "If you make a basket, you move to the next spot. You keep shooting until you miss," Coach said. "When you miss, you have a choice. You can stay in your spot and let the other player shoot. Or you can say 'Risk.' If you risk, you shoot again. If you make the risk basket, you move to the next spot. If you miss, you go home, back to spot one. The winner is the first shooter to move through all ten spots—that's five going out and five coming back. I expect <u>exemplary</u> behavior, Kevin, not the kind I've been seeing from you lately."

16   "Babies, I mean ladies, first," Kevin said to Mary Ruth as he looked around to see if any of his friends had caught his joke. Coach Taggart was at Kevin's side in an instant. "Okay, okay," Kevin said, backing off. He didn't want to get thrown out and miss this chance to beat Mary Ruth.

17   Maybe it was the way Mary Ruth played that silenced Kevin. His insults stopped <u>temporarily</u>. She made the side shots while Kevin missed them. Mary Ruth got halfway "around the world" before Kevin left the home spot for good. At spot three he blew a shot, then "risked," missed, and had to start over. Kevin was stuck at spot two when Mary Ruth got to spot seven.

18   Mary Ruth dribbled and spun in a <u>three-quarter pivot</u>, her left side to the basket. A three-quarter pivot can be tricky. It's when you spin three-quarters of the way around on one foot while positioning the other foot and getting your hand and the ball in the right place all at the same time. But she did it. She launched a hook shot over her head from her right arm. The ball banged off the backboard and <u>rebounded</u> back at her. Kevin laughed nervously.

19   "Risk," Mary Ruth said. She stood very still for a minute, and then fired a jump shot. The ball tipped into the basket from the rim.

20   Mary Ruth missed her shot at spot eight. She passed the ball to Kevin.

21   Kevin landed baskets from the two spots near the center of the half-circle. Once he got to spot five on the far side of the basket, Kevin got into trouble again. He was <u>stalled</u> at spot five when Mary Ruth landed baskets eight, nine, and ten. Mary Ruth beat Kevin at Around the World.

22   The room was quiet. Every kid in the class stood still, watching to see what Kevin would do with the <u>defeat</u>; he wasn't used to losing. His mouth opened. "Why don't you go back to the freak planet you came from," he yelled.

23   Mary Ruth gazed at him. Her eyes traveled around the room, taking in the stares of all the other kids. Quietly, she turned away and walked out of the school.

24   No one really knew where she went after that. She just never showed up at school again. Someone else sat in her desk. Kevin was never quite as popular after that.

25   But fifteen years later she's easy to find. Open any sports page. Turn on any sports channel. Look inside any *Sports Illustrated.* And you'll find her, front and center on the basketball court: star player, Mary Ruth Dunlap.

Basketball Pivot

A

SKILL USING CONTEXT CLUES | **STRATEGY** VOCABULARY DEVELOPMENT: CONTEXT CLUES

Directions: Study and learn the following types of context clues.

Definition/Explanation Clues

Writers will sometimes provide a definition or explanation of a word in the same sentence in which the word appears.

> Example: A _definition_ *tells or explains exactly what a word means.*

In that sentence, the word *definition* is defined. Readers learn what a definition is when they read the sentence.

Restatement/Synonym Clues

Sometimes writers restate difficult words with easier ones, or they give synonyms—words with the same or nearly the same meaning.

> Example: *Jack is interested in _horticulture_, especially in how to grow oversized vegetables.*

In this sentence, the signal word *especially* tells you that an example of horticulture is about to be given. Once you reach the restatement, you understand that *horticulture* is the science of how to grow plants.

Contrast/Antonym Clues

Contrast/Antonym clues give the opposite meaning of an unfamiliar word.

> Example: *He should have _hurtled_ ahead, but instead he stood frozen in place.*

The word *hurtled*, which means "moving at great speed," is defined by its antonym, or opposite, at the end of the sentence: "stood frozen in place." The signal words *but* and *instead* let you know that an opposite meaning is about to appear.

Common Signal Words

Signal words are often found with restatement/synonym and contrast/antonym clues. They point out an explanation or an opposite meaning. Here are some frequently used signal words:

Restatement/Synonym

for example	especially
these	like
such as	so . . . that

Contrast/Antonym

on the other hand	although
still	however
despite	by contrast
not	while

Inference/General Context Clues

Inference or general context clues aren't as obvious as other types of clues. The writer expects you to infer the meaning of an unfamiliar word by thinking about the relationship between the word and other information in the text. These clues may even be a few sentences away from the unfamiliar word.

> Example: *The aging house stood isolated and _decrepit_. The roof sagged and most of the windows were broken. The once beautiful gardens were choked with thorny brambles. For years no living thing had entered the front door.*

Even though no definition, synonym, or antonym is given, you can still figure out what *decrepit* means by thinking about the other information in the passage. The details in the passage tell you that no one had kept up the house; therefore, you can infer that *decrepit* means run down or worn out.

ELEMENTS OF LITERATURE

Mini Read

Basketball Pivot

B

Directions: On the lines provided, identify the type of context clue given for the underlined word in each sentence below: definition/explanation clue, restatement/synonym clue, contrast/antonym clue, or inference/general context clue. Then, based on those context clues and your own ideas, write the meaning of the underlined word.

1. **compressed**

   The best trick I saw last night at the magic show happened when the magician <u>compressed</u> his entire body like a pretzel into a small wooden box.

Context Clue(s): ....

Meaning of Underlined Word: ....

2. **jeered**

   Kevin and the other boys <u>jeered</u> at Mary on the court. Mary, however, seemed to ignore their insults as she made a rebound and scored two points.

Context Clue(s): ....

Meaning of Underlined Word: ....

3. **routine**

   The operation was very <u>routine</u>, a regular procedure. The doctor had performed it many times before.

Context Clue(s): ....

Meaning of Underlined Word: ....

4. **minuscule**

   In the museum, the giant skeleton of the *Tyrannosaurus rex* towered over everything. It made the skeleton of the prehistoric bird look <u>minuscule</u> by comparison.

Context Clue(s): ....

Meaning of Underlined Word: ....

5. **strutted**

   During lunch, Eric proudly <u>strutted</u> from the salad bar to our lunch table, as if on a catwalk for a fashion show. He had just been named student council president. From the way he casually but arrogantly walked through the cafeteria, you would have thought he had been named president of the United States.

Context Clue(s): ....

Meaning of Underlined Word: ....

ELEMENTS OF LITERATURE

The All-American Slurp

SKILL USING CONTEXT CLUES | **STRATEGY** VOCABULARY DEVELOPMENT: CONTEXT CLUES

Directions: Read the sentences below. First, write down the context clues, if any, that the writer gives you so that you can figure out the meanings of these words. Then, write down what type of context clue is used in the sentence. Refer to Blackline Master A (page 42) as a guide for identifying the four types of context clues. The writer may give you one of the following clues:

1. Defining the word within the sentence (definition/explanation clue)
2. Restating the word with an easier one (restatement/synonym clue)
3. Putting the word that means the opposite in the sentence (contrast/antonym clue)
4. Giving information that you can use to infer the word's meaning (inference/general context clue)

Example: He felt so much <u>remorse</u> for what he had done that he confessed to the crime.
Context Clue Words: *You can tell that he felt bad about what he had done, or he wouldn't have confessed. Remorse must mean "feeling guilty."*

Type of Context Clue(s): *inference/general context*

1. lavishly

The TV star's house was decorated <u>lavishly</u>, with more than enough chairs, couches, and dining tables to make one hundred guests feel spoiled and pampered.

Context Clue Words: ....

Type of Context Clue(s): ....

2. mortified

After Paul made that embarrassing mistake, he was not calm; he was <u>mortified</u>.

Context Clue Words: ....

Type of Context Clue(s): ....

3. spectacle

The movie *They Came from Xectron 3* is a remarkable <u>spectacle</u> featuring many colorful explosions and action-packed battles between space aliens and the people of Earth.

Context Clue Words: ....

Type of Context Clue(s): ....

4. sultry

I couldn't believe it when Sheena said, "This <u>sultry</u> weather sure is strange for February." Didn't she see that the back porch was still slick with ice, and the thermometer was reading 33 degrees?

Context Clue Words: ....

Type of Context Clue(s): ....

The Playoff

1   Nicole was a bench warmer—at least, that's what she called herself. This position was quite a change from being the star forward on the field hockey team back home in Massachusetts. She had joined the volleyball team when she moved with her family last fall because they didn't have a girls' field hockey team here. In fact, hardly anybody in this part of the country knew what field hockey was. Nicole figured that maybe some of her other skills might flow over into volleyball. Field hockey, volleyball—what's the difference? Nicole soon found out that some things, like working together, were the same, but running down a field pushing a ball with a stick was very different from using your arms and hands to hit a ball over a net. Even though Nicole had been playing on the varsity team back home, she hardly ever got to play in games here. "Why can't they have a field hockey team here?" Nicole often thought. "Then they could see what I can do."

2   One advantage of joining the team was meeting Tina, her best friend. Tina was the star of the junior varsity team, a natural athlete who couldn't get enough of volleyball. Tina spent her summers going to sports camps and playing in the city league, which was made up of the best volleyball players in town. This year Coach Owens wanted to move Tina to varsity, but the coach was afraid that the junior varsity team might not be any good without Tina.

3   Sometimes it bothered Nicole to think that if she were back in Massachusetts, she'd be playing in every game as a starting player. Here, she felt more like a fan than a teammate. Even though Nicole never missed practice and seemed to be improving, her newness to the sport made Coach Owens reluctant to put her in most of the games. However, one afternoon, a week before the district playoffs, Nicole's chance to play came rather unexpectedly.

4   "Aggh!" Tina cried as she landed after spiking the ball over the net at practice that afternoon.

The Playoff (cont'd)

5   Everyone crowded around Tina as she sat on the gym floor, gripping her ankle. "I think I did something bad to it. It really hurts!" cried Tina. Tina's ankle swelled to grapefruit-size in less than an hour, even with ice packs and elevation. When her doctor checked it out, he said Tina had badly sprained her ankle, and she needed to stop all activity for a month to let it heal.

6   At practice the next day, Coach Owens announced how Tina's injury would affect the team. "I know you are all worried about what we're going to do without Tina, especially since the playoffs are a week away. Now is the time when we really need to band together and push ourselves. To take Tina's place, I'm going to rotate in some of you that haven't played that much this season. So don't panic—just concentrate and make every practice count."

7   When Coach Owens finished speaking, the hairs on Nicole's neck started to tingle from her excitement and fear. She had exactly one week to push herself to learn as many plays as she could. On one hand, Nicole saw this as her chance to prove to everyone, including Tina, that she was a good athlete. On the other hand, what if she was good only at one sport?

* * *

8   That week flew by as Nicole woke up early for drills and went to daily after-school practice, staying until she was the only one left in the gym. Nicole left only when the custodians turned out the lights to let her know it was time to leave.

9   By Friday, Nicole's forearms were red and bruised from all the bumping she had done, and her legs ached from kneeling and jumping to spike and set. Her serves made it over the net only half of the time. Nine times out of ten, she would miss a save during practice, but her teammates and Coach Owens encouraged her to keep trying. She felt motivated by her old feelings of fear and excitement, as well as a desire to play and feel the way she did when she played field hockey. Nicole knew what she was made of—but she wasn't sure others would see it, or whether she could find it in herself in time for the playoff game.

10   Doubts about how well she would play crowded Nicole's thoughts the night before the game and kept her up most of the night. On Friday morning, Nicole felt more ready for a week in bed than an afternoon on the volleyball court.

11   Her team realized that if they wanted to win, they would have to cover for Nicole. Whenever the ball even came close to Nicole, someone else always seemed to be there to make a perfect set or save. Soon the other team noticed their obvious attempts to keep the ball away from Nicole. The other team's coach called a quick timeout. They huddled and made their plan. Pinpointing Nicole as the weak link, they began to make sure the ball went close or right to Nicole on almost every play.

12   For Nicole, halftime seemed hours away as she tried to bump balls to other teammates. Soon the buzzer signaled the end of the first half, and Nicole quickly sat at the far end of the bench, away from the other players. Tina came over on her crutches and carefully sat by Nicole, handing her a drink.

13   "Hey, you look great out there!" said Tina.

14   Nicole turned to Tina and caught her smile. "Don't lie, Tina. You know, the whole team knows, our opponents even know, that I'm the weak link," Nicole said. Then, under her breath, she muttered, "If only this were a field hockey match . . ."

15   "Well, I guess field hockey isn't the same as volleyball," said Tina. "If only I hadn't twisted my ankle, I'd be playing and we would win for sure. Well, only half a game left, and then the game will be over and so will any chance of our advancing to the next level." As Tina stood up on her crutches and went back to the other end of the bench, Nicole's heart beat faster and her face flushed with anger. Tina's lack of confidence in her made Nicole decide not to give up. At that moment, Nicole realized that holding back and not putting her heart into the game made her look less skilled than she really was. Before the buzzer sounded, Nicole was up and on the court.

16   Throughout the second half, the team managed to keep the score tied. A few times Nicole's teammates tried to cover

for her, but the other team kept sending every serve and return her way. Yet, instead of missing volleys or serving into the net, Nicole seemed like a different person out on the court. Was she just so angry that she wanted to prove herself, even at the risk of being embarrassed? With minutes left in the game, the score was still tied. When the other team lobbed the ball swiftly over the net, it made a straight line for Nicole. Without flinching, she quickly clasped her hands together as the ball bombed toward her.

* * *

17   Minutes later, Nicole sat on the bench with one elbow wrapped in ice.

18   "We won, thanks to your great save!" said one of her teammates.

19   "Thanks to your bump, we were able to set and spike it right back to them, which they weren't expecting. Good team-work, Nicole," said Coach Owens. Nicole was in a state of happy shock. She didn't know exactly what had happened once the ball made contact with her arms, but seconds after that, she fell backward onto the wooden floor, her elbow tak-ing the force of her fall. Now her arm hurt so badly she want-ed to cry, but she felt more like laughing.

20   As her teammates started to walk to the locker room to change, they gave her combined looks of surprise and respect, pats on the back, and a few high fives. When Nicole joined her teammates on the way back to the locker room, she met Tina near the locker-room door.

21   "Hey, once your ankle's better, how about helping me start a field hockey team? I don't think this school can handle two volleyball stars," said Nicole, with a huge smile on her face.

The Playoff

Part 1. Directions:

A. Before reading the MiniRead "The Playoff," read the following statements. Decide whether you agree or disagree with each statement. Mark an X in the appropriate blank in the *Before Reading* column, and be ready to explain your decisions. Then, on the lines below the statements, make a prediction about what you think the story will generally be about.

BEFORE READING		AFTER READING
Agree / Disagree	Statement	Agree / Disagree
_____ / _____	1. If you aren't good at something, you shouldn't do it.	_____ / _____
_____ / _____	2. It's better not to do something than to risk looking foolish.	_____ / _____
_____ / _____	3. To prove yourself to others, you have to take risks.	_____ / _____
_____ / _____	4. A sense of competition comes from within.	_____ / _____

My Prediction About the Story: ....

....

B. After reading "The Playoff," mark an X in the appropriate blank in the *After Reading* column to show whether or not your views were influenced by the MiniRead.

Part 2. Directions: On the lines provided, choose three of the Anticipation Guide statements above and describe how each one relates to the story. See the example for the first statement below.

Example: If you aren't good at something, you shouldn't do it.

> *At the beginning of the story, Nicole is better at field hockey than at volleyball.*
> *After practicing and trying her best, she was able to help her team win the playoff.*

1. ....

....

2. ....

....

3. ....

....

ELEMENTS OF LITERATURE

La Bamba

Part 1. Directions:

A. Before you read "La Bamba" (Pupil's Edition, page 44), read each of the following statements and decide if you agree or disagree with the statement. Mark your choice in the appropriate blank for each statement in the *Before Reading* column. Be prepared to explain your decisions. Then, on the lines below the statements, make a prediction about what you think the story generally will be about.

BEFORE READING		AFTER READING
Agree / Disagree	Statement	Agree / Disagree
_____ / _____	1. Accidents always ruin everything.	_____ / _____
_____ / _____	2. Not everyone can be good at something.	_____ / _____
_____ / _____	3. If you take risks, you will always succeed.	_____ / _____
_____ / _____	4. High expectations will always bring disappointment.	_____ / _____

My Prediction About the Story: ....

....

B. After reading "La Bamba," mark an X in the appropriate blank in the *After Reading* column to show whether or not your views were influenced by the story.

Part 2. Directions: Choose three of the Anticipation Guide statements above. On the lines provided, describe how each statement you chose relates to the story.

1. ....

....

....

2. ....

....

....

3. ....

....

....

Beanie Baby™ Madness

1   Eleven major league baseball teams gave them to young fans at special promotional games. U.S. Customs will seize them if you try to bring more than one into the country. There are over one million sites for them on the Internet. It's the big craze of the late 1990s: collecting Beanie Babies™.

2   What's so special about Beanie Babies™? They're just stuffed animals, made in factories like any other stuffed animal. They aren't antiques, because they just came out in 1994. When they're new, they cost only five to eight dollars. And they're not very useful, except as playthings. Since many of their owners are adults, some Beanies spend their lives sitting in boxes.

3   But a lot of people will do almost anything to get the Beanie Babies™ they want. That's because the maker of Beanie Babies™, Ty Inc., understands something about collectors. The most valuable objects in a collection are the scarce ones. The baseball card that's missing from nearly everyone's collection becomes the one that everyone wants. A stamp design that was printed only once becomes hard to find. As a result, the price goes up.

4   Knowing this, Ty Inc. did something very clever. They brought out several different kinds of Beanie Babies™ at a time. They didn't make huge numbers of them. Then they started "retiring" earlier kinds of Beanie Babies™. That is, they simply stopped making them. This shortage caused customers to want the toys even more. The "retired" Beanies became harder to find, so they became valuable to people who had started collecting the toys. Shoppers went wild for new Beanies, too, because they figured that the new ones would later become retired ones.

Special

**Brontosaurus
only
$900.00!**

5   People became so anxious to get their hands on certain Beanies that some Beanies brought in crazy prices. A Bronty the Brontosaurus from 1995 could sell in 1998 for $900. Peanut the Elephant was once mistakenly made in royal blue instead of light blue—so a royal-blue Peanut could sell for $3,500, just because there weren't very many of them.

6   But not every royal-blue Peanut the Elephant could sell for that amount. Woe to the parent who bought a royal-blue Peanut for six dollars in 1995, cut off the tag, and handed the stuffed animal to a four-year-old. That's because the condition of a Beanie has a lot to do with its value. A missing tag can reduce its value by half. A worn-out Beanie is worth much less than the same Beanie in excellent shape.

7   Because of their value to collectors, many Beanies spend their lives in boxes, untouched by children's hands. That's also why it's adults crowding the toy and gift shops. They're often shopping for their own collections, not for their children. The demand is so great that many shops can't keep enough Beanies in stock.

8   Of course, that's the idea. Ty Inc. limits the number of Beanies they will ship to a store each month. The company knows that shortage is the main reason collectors care so much about Beanies. Also, Beanies are not sold in large chain stores. They're usually found in small shops. This placement makes the supply even more difficult to predict.

9   This situation is really just a basic lesson in economics. It's the law of supply and demand. Things that are hard to get are often the things people want most. Store windows often put up signs that read "No More Beanies" or "New Beanies arriving tomorrow," or "We've got Beanies!" Parents have often lined up just to get that one special Beanie their child wanted. Kids have spent hours surfing the Internet to discover what is new and what is retired. Beanie Baby™ buyers know to look for Beanies in small stores instead of huge chain stores.

10   So, if a company can get people interested in a line of stuffed animals and then take some of the animals away, people just might want those missing toys very badly—badly enough to pay quite a lot of money for them.

NAME   CLASS   DATE

Beanie Baby™ Madness

SKILL SUMMARIZING | **STRATEGY** SOMEBODY WANTED BUT SO

Directions: After you read the MiniRead "Beanie Baby™ Madness," complete each of the following Somebody Wanted But So statements.

Somebody	Wanted	But	So
1. Collectors in general			
2. People interested in Beanie Babies™			
3. The owner of a worn-out, royal-blue Peanut the Elephant			

4. Look at your completed statements from the chart above. Which statement offers the best summary of the MiniRead? Explain your answer on the lines below.

....

....

....

Copyright © by Holt, Rinehart and Winston. All rights reserved.

ELEMENTS OF LITERATURE   Active Reader's Practice Book | 31

President Cleveland, Where Are You?

SKILL SUMMARIZING | **STRATEGY** SOMEBODY WANTED BUT SO

Directions: After you read "President Cleveland, Where Are You?" (Pupil's Edition, page 53), complete each of the following Somebody Wanted But So statements.

Somebody	Wanted	But	So
1. The boys collecting cowboy cards			
2. Jerry, just before his father's birthday			
3. Rollie Tremaine, while collecting President cards			
4. Armand, before the dance			
5. Jerry, upon finding out where to get a Grover Cleveland card			

6. Which statement do you think best summarizes the story as a whole? Explain your choice on the lines provided.

....

....

....

....

....

ELEMENTS OF LITERATURE

A Ledge to Grind On

1   In spite of the midday summer heat, the Wheeler brothers and their friend Brian had made up their minds to find a new grinding ledge somewhere in the neighborhood. John and Brian were already wearing their in-line skates. With his mom at work, John could ignore her "no skates in the house" rule. He'd just slide into the kitchen to grab a bottle of water.

2   Anthony, who didn't feel as skilled on in-line skates as the other two, took his skateboard along. Summertime was good. You could sleep as late as you wanted most days, watch TV and play video games, walk to the hamburger or taco place for lunch, and go swimming when the heat got too bad. Anthony had planned to get a job this summer doing the only thing that a fourteen-year-old could do: sacking groceries at the nearby supermarket. A lot of other kids thought of the same thing, and by the time he got around to applying in mid-June, the store wasn't hiring any more summer help.

3   John, who was a year younger than Anthony, was really into the skate scene. He'd been to a real skatepark in Dallas. The only real place to skate here was a makeshift skatepark inside a building on the far south side of town. It was not in a convenient location, and it cost ten dollars to get in. The skaters liked the rails and ledges at the neighborhood elementary school, but construction fences closed off the place for the summer. Sometimes the boys went downtown to banks and parking garages that had steps for practicing spins. But downtown was so far away, and it was so hot outside.

4   Brian, who liked to be the best at everything he did, stayed at his mother's house every other week. Whenever he stayed at his mother's, he spent most of his time at the Wheelers'. There was always something to do there, and his mom and stepfather didn't seem to mind.

5   About three blocks from the Wheelers' house, the three boys discovered the ledge. It had always been there, of course; they'd just never thought of it in terms

of skating. It was a foot-tall concrete curb that marked the entrance to a block of small, older homes. As they skated out of the house to the ledge, the boys grabbed their helmets and strapped them on, then quickly secured their kneepads to their moving legs. Once they reached their new skate area, John started off with a *unity*, a cross-legged grind, and Brian followed. They looked up to see a tall, thin, gray-haired woman standing on her porch. She just stared at the boys, not saying a word. They ignored her, but after a few minutes, John scraped his elbow doing a soul grind. So it was back to the house for some quick first aid, elbow pads, and more water.

6   When the boys returned to the curb, the sun was orange and low on the horizon. "I've got to get this soul grind right," said John as he jumped up, the outside of his boot on the ledge. Suddenly, a screen door flew open and the old woman came running down the porch steps. "Why are you doing that on my wall?" she called out in an unfamiliar British accent. "Why don't you go home and do that on your own wall? Look at you; look at how you are dressed! What part of town do you come from? Why don't you go home?" She shook her fist and seemed about to cry.

7   "We're your neighbors," John mumbled under his breath. But as he began his final grind, something went wrong. His foot turned, there was a cracking sound, and he was lying on the side-walk, grabbing his knee. "Oh, man, I hurt my knee," John moaned. The old lady moved closer, bent down, felt his knee, and frowned. Then everything began to happen at once. Standing up, she ordered Brian into the house to call 911. She quizzed Anthony about his parents' work numbers. When Brian returned shouting, "They're on their way," she sent him back in to make the other calls. In a short time, the ambulance crew, the Wheeler parents, and curious neighbors were surrounding the fallen skater, who looked pale, almost greenish. As the ambulance took off, the woman turned to Brian and Anthony and ordered, "Come into the house for a drink. It's much too hot to be standing out here."

8   The boys looked at each other. They couldn't think of an excuse to leave, so they found themselves in the unlikely position of sitting in the woman's dark living room and drinking watery lemonade. The woman just wouldn't stop talking. "I had just gotten out of nursing school in London and wanted to do something to help. But it was so hard; so many lovely boys, so badly hurt." Anthony raised his eyebrows and looked at Brian.

9   "She must be talking about World War II," Brian said under his breath. "You know, we talked about it in English class when we read about Anne Frank."

10   "Then it was over, and there were the most wonderful celebrations. Parades, parties, so many Americans! That's how I met Charlie—not just a good-looking Yank, but a Texan!" The boys started squirming, and her voice got lower. "It's hard to believe it's been almost two years that he's been gone."

11   "Well, we really have to go, Mrs., er. . . ," began Brian.

12   "Clark," she replied. "Abigail Clark. Charlie and I lived on this corner for forty years."

13   "Thanks for helping my brother," Anthony said. They all stood in the doorway a moment, but no one had anything else to say.

14   Anthony awoke before the sun was up the next morning. He felt something was different, and then he remembered: John wasn't on the bottom bunk. Mom and Dad would soon be going to the hospital for the surgery. John would be out of the skate scene for the rest of the summer, and Anthony would probably have to wait on him as he sat in his cast in front of the computer.

15   Stopping in the kitchen for a banana, Anthony went to the garage, pulled out the lawn mower, and began pushing it slowly down the street. Mrs. Clark's lawn looked as if it could use a mowing.

A Ledge to Grind On

SKILL MAKING GENERALIZATIONS | **STRATEGY** IT SAYS . . . I SAY

Directions: After you read the MiniRead "A Ledge to Grind On," read the questions below. Reread the story for information that helps answer each question, and put that information in the *It Says* column. Then, in the *I Say* column, write your own thoughts on the matter. Add any outside information that you think is important. Then, in the *And So* column, use the comments from the *It Says* and *I Say* columns to make a generalization.

Question	It Says . . . (What the text says)	I Say . . . (My thoughts)	And So . . . (My generalizations)
1. After reading "A Ledge to Grind On," what can you say about judging people based on first impressions?			
2. After reading "A Ledge to Grind On," what generalization can you make about being open to changing opinions?			
3. After reading "A Ledge to Grind On," what can you say about relationships between older people and younger people?			

ELEMENTS OF LITERATURE

The Stone

Directions: After you read "The Stone" (Pupil's Edition, page 69), read the questions below. Reread the story for information that helps answer each question, and put that information in the *It Says* column. Then, in the *I Say* column, write your own thoughts on the matter. Add any outside information that you think is important. Then, in the *And So* column, use your comments from the *It Says* and *I Say* columns to make a generalization.

Question	It Says ... (What the text says)	I Say ... (My thoughts)	And So ... (My generalizations)
1. After reading "The Stone," what can you say about wishes?			
2. After reading "The Stone," what can you say about making good decisions?			
3. After reading "The Stone," what can you say about the importance of change?			

ELEMENTS OF LITERATURE

Storm *from* Woodsong

SKILL MONITORING COMPREHENSION | **STRATEGY** SAY SOMETHING

Part 1. Directions: Decide with a partner whether you will read "Storm" (Pupil's Edition, page 96) silently or aloud. As you read, pause at places in the text you have both agreed are "stopping places" (perhaps every two or three paragraphs), and take turns saying something about what you just read. In the appropriate column of the chart below, write a checkmark for each type of comment you make.

Prediction	Comment	Question	Connection

Part 2. Directions: Think about the Say Something dialogue you had with your partner, and answer the following questions on the lines provided.

1. If someone had been listening in on your Say Something dialogue, what would he or she have heard? Give a summary. ....

....

2. Did you answer any questions for your partner? Did your partner answer any questions for you? What were they? What questions remain unanswered? ....

....

3. What type of comment did you make the most, based on your chart above? Why do you think you made that type of comment the most? ....

....

4. How did the Say Something strategy help you monitor your comprehension of the selection?

....

5. If you were to do a Say Something again, how would you do it differently? ....

....

Brothers Forever

1   Imagine having a brother who was always grouchy, hardly ever bathed, had a horrible temper, and sometimes did wild things without thinking them through. How would you deal with him? Theo van Gogh had a brother like this, and his name was Vincent. Even though Vincent seems like a brother who was hard to deal with, Theo overlooked all of Vincent's faults and accepted him—like a brother.

2   Vincent and Theo's respect and loyalty for each other had no limits. Theo paid the way for his artist brother Vincent, and Vincent never paid the money back. Instead, he gave Theo hundreds of paintings that were worthless at that time.

3   Vincent sold only one painting during his entire life, and almost everyone but Theo thought his artworks were bad. Some people burned Vincent's paintings like firewood and used them to patch holes in chicken coops and outdoor bathrooms. Today, the beauty and value of Vincent van Gogh's paintings stun the world. In 1990, his portrait of a doctor sold—in less than three minutes—for more than eighty million dollars. Vincent and his brother Theo never received even a little bit of these riches.

4   To some of us, Theo's loyalty to Vincent may be hard to understand. As a brother and as a human being, Vincent was unusual. He did not like to bathe. Vincent's teeth were rotten—he had to have ten of them yanked out. He wore dirty old clothes and proudly called himself a "shaggy dog." The way he dressed could be described as unstylish and weird—one suit he made and wore had yellow polka dots on a bright purple background.

5   Vincent's personality was odd, too. He constantly fought with everyone, even the brother he loved. Friends also feared Vincent's temper—for good reasons. In a famous episode, Vincent was so angry at his friend, artist Paul Gauguin, that he almost slashed Gauguin with a razor. Later, Vincent cut off his own ear to pun-

ish himself. He then delivered the ear, wrapped like a little present, to a female friend.

6   Even people who hardly knew Vincent avoided him. In a village where he lived near the end of his life, a crowd frequently shouted "redheaded fool!" beneath his window. He yelled back and threw his paintings at them. Soon the town's residents signed a petition demanding that Vincent be put in a mental health hospital.

7   During his lifetime, Vincent was poor and used his monthly allowance from Theo to buy art supplies, often running out of money for food. Sometimes Vincent didn't eat for days so that he could buy paints and canvas. Usually he lived on coffee, bread, and cheese; if he grew hungry between meals, he licked his brushes. It's not an exaggeration to say that Vincent actually lived, breathed, and ate his work. In fact, despite his troubles and visits to the hospital, Vincent painted nonstop. Two of his most famous artworks, *Starry Night* and *Irises*, were of the view from the window of a hospital.

8   Vincent could maintain this love for art because of Theo. You could say that Theo's brotherly support not only kept Vincent going, but also gave the world one of the greatest painters ever known. When they were apart, Theo and Vincent wrote each other every week and sometimes twice a day. Their letters are full of kind words and shared respect for each other.

9   In 1890, when Vincent died at age thirty-seven, his last letter to Theo was in his pocket. Theo could not bear Vincent's absence and died of natural causes just six months later. Sunflowers—the subject of many of Vincent's paintings for Theo—were planted on both brothers' graves. Within thirty years, Vincent van Gogh was famous all over the world.

| NAME | CLASS | DATE |

Brothers Forever

SKILL DETERMINING THE MAIN IDEA | **STRATEGY** SAVE THE LAST WORD FOR ME

Part 1. Directions: After reading the MiniRead "Brothers Forever," choose your favorite passage and copy it on the lines provided.

"

....

....

....

....

....

....

....

....

"

Part 2. Directions: On the lines provided, answer the following questions.

1. Why did you choose this passage?

....

....

....

2. How does this passage reflect important ideas in "Brothers Forever"?

....

....

....

....

ELEMENTS OF LITERATURE

Brother

SKILL DETERMINING THE MAIN IDEA | **STRATEGY** SAVE THE LAST WORD FOR ME

Part 1. Directions: After reading "Brother" (Pupil's Edition, page 109), choose your favorite passage and copy it on the lines provided.

"

....

....

....

....

....

....

....

....

....

....

"

Part 2. Directions: On the lines provided, answer the following questions.

1. Why did you choose this passage?

....

....

....

2. How does this passage reflect important ideas in "Brother"?

....

....

....

....

ELEMENTS OF LITERATURE

The *Amistad* Chronicles

EXTRA!!! The Times EXTRA!!!

SUPREME COURT RULES THAT *AMISTAD* CAPTIVES ARE FREE

Court Says That Africans Held for Almost Two Years Are Victims of Kidnapping

1   WASHINGTON, D.C. MARCH 9, 1841—Today, the United States Supreme Court decided on the case of the *Amistad* captives. After almost two years of trials, the *Amistad* captives are free to return to Africa. Former president and current congressman John Quincy Adams argued to uphold what the lower courts had decided—that the *Amistad* captives were not guilty of murder and that they were not slaves.

2   The Africans had been accused of murdering two of the men transporting them onboard the Spanish ship. The ship and its passengers were held by the U.S. Navy when it landed on the coast of Long Island, New York, in August of 1839. When Spain asked that the ship and the Africans be returned to Cuba, U.S. officials decided to hold a trial of the *Amistad* captives in the United States.

3   According to the freed defendants, the story of the thirty-seven men and four children who have become known as the *Amistad* captives began over two years ago. Kidnapped from their native country of Sierra Leone in January of 1839, the Africans were taken across the Atlantic Ocean to Cuba against their will. "We were treated horribly," said one. "The slave traders kept us in chains and beat us. We were allowed up on deck only once a day."

4   In Havana, the captives were sold to Ramon Ferrer and placed on the slave ship *Amistad.* On their way to another Cuban city, the Africans, led by a man named Sengbe, were able to free themselves from their chains and overtake the crew. The captain and the ship's cook were killed. Some sailors escaped, and the Africans let two sailors live in order to guide the ship to Africa, the captives' homeland.

EXTRA!!! The Times EXTRA!!!

5   Instead, the navigator sailed the ship north to the United States, and Sengbe was arrested when he and others went ashore for food and water.

6   Since then a battle has been fought in the courts. It has been closely followed by the nation's abolitionist groups, those opposed to slavery. Today's ruling was based on the fact that it has been illegal since 1808 to bring people into the United States to be slaves. This ruling upheld the lower court decision that, as kidnapping victims, the Sierra Leoneans had the right to escape any way they could.

7   The group will return to Sierra Leone as soon as the former captives can raise the funds for the trip.

AMISTAD CAPTIVES ARRIVE HOME

8   FREETOWN, SIERRA LEONE, AFRICA, 1842—Anxious friends and relatives were at the docks today to greet the returning *Amistad* captives. Away from home for three years, the prisoners, led by Sengbe from the Mende tribe, were released after several trials in the United States. In March of 1841, they were found not guilty of murder and declared free by the U.S. Supreme Court. Funds for the trip back to Africa were raised by American abolitionist groups.

9   The men and children, kidnapped in 1839, were shipped under terrible conditions to Cuba, where they managed to escape from their chains and take over the Spanish ship *Amistad*. In the course of the uprising, two of their captors were killed. Trying to return to Sierra Leone, the captives instead landed on the eastern coast of the United States. In the Supreme Court trial, former United States president John Quincy Adams argued in their defense.

10   Bringing slaves into the country has been illegal in the United States since 1808. It is still legal to bring slaves into Cuba.

The *Amistad* Chronicles

SKILL USING CHRONOLOGY | **STRATEGY** RETELLINGS

Part 1. Directions: As you read the MiniRead "The *Amistad* Chronicles," write down on the lines provided any signal words or phrases that indicate sequence or chronology (time order). Continue on the back of this sheet if necessary. Use these words and others you think of when doing your retelling. [**Example:** *today, when it landed*]

....

....

....

Part 2. Directions: Decide who will retell the first MiniRead article and who will listen to and score the retelling. The listener should score the retelling on the reteller's rating chart, using the questions and scale below. A *0* on the scale means the reteller didn't include the item at all; a *3* means the reteller answered the question completely. When you are finished with the first retelling, silently read the second article in the MiniRead. Then switch roles, retelling and rating the retelling for the second article. Be sure to retell events in each article chronologically, as they are presented in the MiniRead.

Retellings Rating Chart   Listener:_____

Does this retelling				
1. have an introduction that includes the MiniRead's title and setting?	0	1	2	3
2. include the main events and people involved?	0	1	2	3
3. keep the main events in correct chronological order?	0	1	2	3
4. provide supporting details?	0	1	2	3
5. make sense?	0	1	2	3
6. sound organized?	0	1	2	3
7. discuss any conflicts or problems that occur in the MiniRead?	0	1	2	3
8. explain how those conflicts/problems are resolved?	0	1	2	3
9. connect the MiniRead to another story or to the reader's life?	0	1	2	3
10. include the reader's personal response to the MiniRead?	0	1	2	3

Total Score: _____

Comments from the listener about the retelling: ....

....

Suggestions for the next retelling: ....

....

A Glory over Everything

Part 1. Directions: As you read "A Glory over Everything" (Pupil's Edition, page 136), write down on the lines provided any signal words that indicate sequence or chronology. Continue on the back of this sheet if necessary. Use these words and others you think of when doing your retelling. [**Example:** *after that*]

....

....

....

Part 2. Directions: First, decide who will retell the beginning of the story and who will listen to and score the retelling. Then, read the first section of the selection, from page 138 to the break in the second column on page 140. One partner should retell that section, and the listener should rate the retelling by using the questions and rating scale below. The listener should score the retelling on the reteller's rating chart. A *0* on the scale means the reteller didn't include the item at all; a *3* means the reteller answered the question completely. When you are finished with the first retelling, read the rest of the selection. Then switch roles, retelling and rating the retelling for the remaining section of "A Glory over Everything." Be sure to keep the events in your retelling in chronological order.

Retellings Rating Chart   Listener:_____

Does this retelling				
1. have an introduction that includes the selection's title and setting?	0	1	2	3
2. include the main events and people involved?	0	1	2	3
3. keep the main events in correct chronological order?	0	1	2	3
4. provide supporting details?	0	1	2	3
5. make sense?	0	1	2	3
6. sound organized?	0	1	2	3
7. discuss any conflicts or problems that occur in the selection?	0	1	2	3
8. explain how those conflicts/problems are resolved?	0	1	2	3
9. connect the selection to another story or to the reader's life?	0	1	2	3
10. include the reader's personal response to the selection?	0	1	2	3

Total Score: _____

Comments from the listener about the retelling: ....

....

Suggestions for the next retelling: ....

The Fun They Had

SKILL ANALYZING CAUSE AND EFFECT | **STRATEGY** TEXT REFORMULATION

Part 1. Directions: After reading "The Fun They Had" (Pupil's Edition, page 204), decide if you will reformulate the story with the *If/Then* pattern or the *Fortunately/Unfortunately* pattern. Brainstorm ideas with two or three classmates. Once you have finished brainstorming, use the space below to write your group's Text Reformulation. (Every group member should write down the reformulation. Continue your reformulation on the back of this sheet if necessary.)

....

....

....

....

....

....

....

....

....

....

Part 2. Directions: Based on your Text Reformulation of "The Fun They Had," answer the following questions.

1. What caused Margie to think about the fun that kids in the past had?

Effect: Margie thinks of the fun they had.

Cause: ....

....

2. What was the effect of Margie having a computer for a teacher?

Cause: Digital teacher

Effect: ....

....

Zlateh the Goat

Directions: Work with a partner to read "Zlateh the Goat" (Pupil's Edition, page 240) and make Think-Aloud comments. One partner should be the reader who reads aloud Pupil's Edition pages 242–243, pausing to make comments, while the listener uses a tally mark to identify those comments in the *Tally* column below. Then, switch roles and continue reading and commenting to the end of the selection.

Think-Aloud Tally Sheet   Listener:_____

Think-Aloud Comments	Tally
Predicting what happens next	
Picturing the text	
Making comparisons	
Identifying problems	
Fixing problems	
Making comments	

Stray

Directions: After you read "Stray" (Pupil's Edition, page 250), read the questions below. Reread the story for information that helps answer each question, and put that information in the *It Says* column. In the *I Say* column, write your own thoughts on the matter. Add any outside information that you think is important. Then, in the *And So* column, combine your comments from the *It Says* and *I Say* columns in order to draw an inference.

Question	It Says ... (What the text says)	I Say ... (My thoughts)	And So ... (My inferences)
1. Why do Doris's parents not say anything when Doris tells them the puppy is good, smart, and not much trouble?			
2. Why doesn't Doris give the puppy a name?			
3. What kind of person is Mr. Lacey?			

ELEMENTS OF LITERATURE

The Flood

Part 1. Directions: As you read "The Flood" (Pupil's Edition, page 263), write down on the lines provided any signal words that indicate sequence or chronology (time order). Continue on the back of this sheet if necessary. Use these words and others you think of when doing your retelling.
[**Example:** *before learning*]

....

....

....

Part 2. Directions: Decide who will retell the first part of the selection and who will score the retelling. One partner should retell "The Flood" from page 268 ("Clarence the cross-eyed lion . . .") to page 271 ("I was having some coffee . . ."). The listener should score the retelling by using the reteller's rating chart. A *0* on the scale means the reteller didn't include the item at all; a 3 means the reteller answered the question completely. When you are done, finish reading the selection silently. Then, switch roles, retelling and rating the retelling for the second section. Be sure to order the events in your retelling chronologically.

Retellings Rating Chart

Listener: _____

Does this retelling				
1. have an introduction that includes the selection's title and setting?	0	1	2	3
2. include the main events and people involved?	0	1	2	3
3. keep the main events in the correct order?	0	1	2	3
4. provide supporting details?	0	1	2	3
5. make sense?	0	1	2	3
6. sound organized?	0	1	2	3
7. discuss any conflicts or problems that occur in the selection?	0	1	2	3
8. explain how those conflicts/problems are resolved?	0	1	2	3
9. connect the selection to another story or to the reader's life?	0	1	2	3
10. include the reader's personal response to the selection?	0	1	2	3

Total Score: _____

Comments from the listener about the retelling: ....

....

Suggestions for the next retelling: ....

....

from The Land I Lost

Directions: After you read the excerpt from "The Land I Lost" (Pupil's Edition, page 280), complete each of the following Somebody/Something Wanted But So statements.

Somebody/ Something	Wanted	But	So
1. Lan, after the wedding			
2. Trung, the first time he heard Lan's cries			
3. Trung's relatives			
4. The crocodile			

5. On the back of this sheet, explain which statement in the above chart offers the best summary of the selection. Be sure to explain your choice.

from All I Really Need to Know I Learned in Kindergarten

SKILL DETERMINING THE MAIN IDEA | **STRATEGY** MOST IMPORTANT WORD

Part 1. Directions: After reading the excerpt from "All I Really Need to Know I Learned in Kindergarten" (Pupil's Edition, page 291), look back through the selection and choose at least three words that you consider important. In the chart below, write each word in the left-hand column. In the right-hand column, explain why you think each word may be the most important. Use examples from the selection to support each word choice.

Important Words	Why This Word is Important in the Selection
1.	
2.	
3.	

Part 2. Directions: Look at the chart above and reread your reasons for each word choice. Then, answer the following questions on the lines provided.

4. After thinking about my word choices, I think the most important word in this selection is

....

5. How does this word reflect important ideas in the selection?

....

....

....

6. Now, using your most important word, write a statement that expresses the main idea of the selection.

....

....

....

The Gold Cadillac

SKILL MAKING PREDICTIONS | **STRATEGY** STORY IMPRESSIONS

Part 1. Directions: Before reading "The Gold Cadillac" (Pupil's Edition page 338), look at the following key words from the story and brainstorm how these words and phrases might be related in a story. Keeping the words in the same order, write your Story Impression on the lines provided.

Key Words
Wilma
↓
father
↓
gold Cadillac
↓
mother angry
↓
trip to the South
↓
policeman
↓
stolen
↓
hid inside
↓
back home

My Story Impression:

....
....
....
....
....
....
....
....
....
....
....
....
....
....
....
....
....

Part 2. Directions: After reading "The Gold Cadillac," review your Story Impression. How close was your prediction to the actual story? On the lines below, explain how your Story Impression was similar to or different from the actual story.

....
....
....

The Bracelet

Skill Making Generalizations | **Strategy** Most Important Word

Part 1. Directions: After reading "The Bracelet" (Pupil's Edition, page 356), make a general statement about one of the following topics:

     a) internment

     b) friendship

     c) what it means to be an American

To help you make your generalization,

   1. From the story, choose one word you think best captures what this story is about.

   2. Next, give some reasons that explain why this word is important.

   3. Then, look at the three topics above and consider the word you chose as most important. What generalized statement can you make?

Part 2. Directions: In small groups, listen to and share the most important words selected by each group member. Discuss the reasons group members give for their choices, especially for those different from your word choice. What do you think of their words and their reasons for choosing them? After you have finished your discussion, answer the following questions on the lines provided.

   4. After the group discussion, I decided that the most important word is ....

   5. I changed/didn't change my mind because: ....

   6. The group discussion has led me to the following generalization(s):

ELEMENTS OF LITERATURE

The Fairy Godmother Failure

Mini-Read

<u>Cast of Characters:</u>

Narrator (Older Emily)	Brother 1	Teacher
Emily	Brother 2	
Fairy godmother	Brother 3	

1   **Narrator:** Once upon a time there was me—Emily. I was miserable. Not just sad or unlucky, but completely and utterly miserable. You would have been miserable, too, if you had been me.

2   For one thing, I had three really rotten older brothers. They pulled my hair when Mom wasn't looking, then pretended that nothing had happened. They stole my CD player and my schoolbooks so that everyone thought I was the most forgetful person in the whole world. They never, I mean never, let me hang out in their treehouse.

3   **Brothers:** Naa, naa, Emily's a girl. No girls allowed.

4   **Emily:** Blockheads!

5   **Narrator:** I was hopeless at school. I lost my homework all the time, even when my brothers didn't steal it. I got horrible grades.

6   **Mom:** Emily, your grades are awful! You are grounded, and you have to clean the whole house.

7   **Narrator:** She especially liked to make me clean the bathroom.

8   **Mom:** And don't forget to clean the bathroom!

9   **Narrator:** Mom never, ever let me do anything fun. The boys could do whatever they wanted, but whenever I asked her . . .

10   **Emily:** Mom, can I go hang gliding?

11   **Mom:** No, dear.

12   **Emily:** Mom, can I go in-line skating?

13   **Mom:** No, dear.

14   **Emily:** Mom, can I climb to the top of the jungle gym?

15   **Mom:** No, Emily, you could break your arm.

16   **Narrator:** Last week was really bad. I woke up late because my alarm clock didn't go off. I wore socks that didn't match, and everyone at the bus stop laughed at me. I went back home to change my socks . . . and I missed the bus. Mom had to drive me, and she wasn't very happy about it.

17   **Mom:** Emily, what am I going to do with you!

18   **Narrator:** I was late to homeroom, and my teacher wasn't very happy about that.

19   **Teacher:** Emily, what am I going to do with you!

20   **Narrator:** It was Thursday, and we had a spelling test. I had forgotten to study my words. Then, we had a pop quiz in science, and I failed it, as usual. My math homework was all wrong. At lunch, my best friend threw up on my shoes. Then, I had to eat by myself. After

school, I ran all the way into the woods so that no one could hear me. I was mad. I was really mad. So I screamed.

21 **Emily:** I AM MISERABLE, I AM MISERABLE! I AM MISERABLE, AND I WISH SOMEONE WOULD COME AND MAKE IT ALL BETTER!

22 **Narrator:** I felt a little bit better, but not much. Then, out of nowhere, an old woman whizzed by me on a pair of roller skates. She ran right into a tree. I helped her up.

23 **Emily:** Are you okay?

24 **Fairy:** Oh dear. . . . Yes, yes, I am fine. Just fine. . . . How are you, Emily?

25 **Emily:** Wait a second, how do you know my name?

26 **Fairy:** Why, I am your fairy godmother! Of course I know your name.

27 **Emily:** My fairy godmother?

28 **Fairy:** Yes, yes, you are miserable, and I am here to help you. That's what you wanted, isn't it? You wished for someone to come and make things all better, didn't you?

29 **Emily:** But . . . you?

30 **Narrator:** She certainly didn't look like your typical fairy godmother. Roller skates, crooked wand, and a hat that definitely had seen better days.

31 **Fairy:** Yes, me. Now, what would you like as your first wish?

32 **Narrator:** I thought of all the things that made me miserable and how I could make them all go away if I had a wish. Maybe this fairy godmother could do some good around here, I thought. Maybe she's just what I need.

33 **Emily:** First, I would like you to make it so that I'm not miserable anymore.

34 **Fairy:** Ohhh dear. Ooohhh dear. Oooooooh—

35 **Emily:** Would you *please* stop saying that?

36 **Narrator:** I was getting tired of her already, and she hadn't even granted my first wish.

37 **Emily:** Now, I've made a wish; you are here to grant wishes. What is the problem?

38 **Fairy:** I—I—I . . . I can't make people happy. It's against the rules. Well, it's pretty much impossible. Isn't there something smaller we could start with? Is there a toy that you want?

39 **Emily:** I'm too old to play with toys, but . . . there is my homework. Fairy godmother, I demand that you do my homework!

40 **Narrator:** She pulled a magic pencil out of her hat, said some magic words, and with a single wave of the magic pencil, my homework was all done. I looked at the homework, and it looked all wrong to me. But what did I know? I was just a little kid, and this was a fairy godmother.

41 **Emily:** Next I would like you to put a spell on my things so that I will never lose them again.

42 **Narrator:** So she pulled a bit of magic dust out of her hat, sprinkled it on my books, and said some magic words. Then there was a great puff of magic smoke, . . . but then, my books were gone.

43 **Emily:** You weren't supposed to make them disappear!

44 **Fairy:** Sorry, sorry dear. That's right. It's abracadabra not cabradabra. Oh dear.

45 **Emily:** Never mind, I have lots of other wishes. Now I want you to make my brothers be nice to me.

46 **Narrator:** We went to the treehouse where my brothers were, and she climbed up and waved her magic wand over them. In the middle of the spell, though, she slipped and fell all the way to the bottom. When my brothers came out, they were frogs!

47 **Emily:** I didn't say to turn them into frogs!

48 **Fairy:** Sorry, so sorry, dear. I must have said it backward again.

49 **Narrator:** I helped her up, and we went home for dinner.

50 **Mom:** Where are your brothers?

51 **Fairy and Emily:** I don't know.

52 **Emily:** Can I keep some pet frogs in my room?

53 **Mom:** Of course not, dear.

54 **Emily:** Then can my fairy godmother sleep over?

55 **Mom:** As long as you finish your homework.
    [Emily shows homework to Mom and Mom nods.]

56 **Emily:** [to Fairy] Tomorrow, while I am at school, I want you to build me a treehouse. It better be the best treehouse in the world, or you're fired.

57 **Fairy:** Oh, dear.

58 **Narrator:** The next day I turned in my homework and my teacher said . . .

59 **Teacher:** This is all wrong. Every single answer. Worse than usual, Emily.

60 **Emily:** But, my fairy godmother did it, and I just thought—

61 **Teacher:** Nonsense! Where are your books?

62 **Emily:** My fairy godmother . . . I mean, I lost them.

63 **Narrator:** When I got home, my parents were really worried about my brothers. They were also not very happy about the frogs in my room. Finally, I went to the forest to see my treehouse. It was a disaster. It was upside down and at the bottom of the tree.

64 **Emily:** This treehouse is upside down and at the bottom of the tree!

65 **Fairy:** Oh, dear . . . Is something wrong, Emily?

66 **Emily:** Yes, something is wrong. Something is definitely, horribly, terribly, miserably wrong. *You* are wrong. *You* are the worst fairy godmother I have ever seen. Cinderella's fairy godmother got her a prince. Sleeping Beauty's fairy godmother saved her life, but *you* . . . you haven't done anything right. You are a fairy godmother failure!

67 **Narrator:** Then my fairy godmother started to cry. It was a miserable sound.

68 **Fairy:** You're right. You're absolutely right. I was never any good at this. Things are worse than they were before. This always happens. I just mess things up worse when I'm sup-

posed to make them better. Oh dear!

69 **Emily:** Things aren't that bad. I'm sure you can fix them. Just get out your spell book and try again.

70 **Fairy:** It's no use. . . . This was my last chance, and when you send me back, that will be it. No wand, no spell book, no magic hat.

71 **Narrator:** I was still mad at her, but I didn't want to see her cry, and I didn't want her to get into trouble.

72 **Narrator and Emily:** Someone had to do something.

73 **Narrator:** I took the treehouse apart, piece by piece, using the hammer and screwdriver. After I finished taking it apart, I rebuilt it in the tree. My fairy godmother helped. I didn't let her put any spells on it, but she was good at handing me wood, and she really liked to help paint. Then I looked up some frog spells and said them backward to turn my frogs back into brothers.

74 **Brothers:** Emily's a freakazoid! I'm going to tell on you!

75 **Narrator:** Sometimes I wish I had left them as frogs.

76 **Emily:** [to brothers] If you ever steal anything again, I will have my fairy godmother turn you into lizards and keep you in little jars on my window sill.

77 **Narrator:** Then I did all my homework over again very carefully. Do you know what?

78 **Emily:** I made a hundred!

79 **Teacher:** Congratulations, Emily!

80 **Narrator:** There was nothing that could be done about the books. I had to get new ones. I also had to pay for the old ones, so I got a job mowing Mrs. Purkapile's yard.

81 **Fairy:** Well, Emily, it looks like you fixed everything!

82 **Emily:** Well, I don't think things are perfect, but they are a lot better than they were.

83 **Fairy:** Are you going to send me back?

84 **Emily:** Do you want to go back?

85 **Fairy:** No, oh dear, nooooo—

86 **Emily:** Then why don't you stay?

87 **Fairy:** Well, I'll never be a very good fairy godmother.

88 **Emily:** That's okay. . . . You're pretty good company. Besides, what would you do without someone like me to take care of you?

"The Fairy Godmother Failure" by Lisa Weckerle.
Copyright© 2000 by Lisa Weckerle.

The Fairy Godmother Failure

SKILL DISTINGUISHING FACT FROM OPINION | **STRATEGY** TEXT REFORMULATION

Part 1. Directions: After reading the MiniRead "The Fairy Godmother Failure," read each of the following statements taken from the text. On the line provided, write *Fact* if the statement is a fact or *Opinion* if it is an opinion. In the space provided, explain your answer.

_____ 1. "For one thing, I had three really rotten older brothers."

Explanation: ....

....

_____ 2. "I wore socks that didn't match, and everyone at the bus stop laughed at me."

Explanation: ....

....

_____ 3. "She certainly didn't look like your typical fairy godmother."

Explanation: ....

....

_____ 4. "You are a fairy godmother failure!"

Explanation: ....

....

_____ 5. "This treehouse is upside down and at the bottom of the tree!"

Explanation: ....

....

_____ 6. "There was nothing that could be done about the books. I had to get new ones. I also had to pay for the old ones, so I got a job mowing Mrs. Purkapile's yard."

Explanation: ....

....

Part 2. Directions: Choose one fact statement and one opinion statement from Part 1. Then, reformulate the fact statement into an opinion statement, and the opinion statement into a fact statement. You might need to add or delete some information to make your reformulation work.

Fact   7. ....

Reformulation: ....

Opinion   8. ....

Reformulation: ....

ELEMENTS OF LITERATURE

The Adventure of the Speckled Band

SKILL DISTINGUISHING FACT FROM OPINION | **STRATEGY** TEXT REFORMULATION

Part 1. Directions: After reading "The Adventure of the Speckled Band" (Pupil's Edition, page 408), read each of the following statements taken from the selection. On the line provided, write *Fact* if the statement is a fact or *Opinion* if it is an opinion. In the space provided, explain your answer.

_____ 1. "There is no mystery, my dear madam. The left arm of your jacket is spattered with mud in no less than seven places. The marks are perfectly fresh. Only a carriage throws up mud in that way." (page 410)

Explanation: ....

....

_____ 2. "I will go when I've had my say. Don't you dare meddle with my affairs. I am a dangerous man to make angry!" (page 417)

Explanation: ....

....

_____ 3. "What a friendly person. I'm not so bulky, but if he had stayed I might have shown him that my grip was not much more feeble than his own." (page 417)

Explanation: ....

....

_____ 4. "The snake provided a type of poison which would not appear on a chemical test, and it would take a very sharp-eyed coroner to notice the two tiny holes where the snake had done its work." (pages 422–423)

Explanation: ....

....

Part 2. Directions: Choose one fact statement and one opinion statement from Part 1. Then, reformulate the fact statement into an opinion statement, and the opinion statement into a fact statement. You might need to add or delete some information to make your reformulation work.

Fact   5. ....

Reformulation: ....

Opinion   6. ....

Reformulation: ....

from Volcano

Part 1. Directions: After reading the excerpt from *Volcano* (Pupil's Edition, page 498), decide if you will reformulate the story into the *If/Then* pattern or the *Fortunately/Unfortunately* pattern. Brainstorm ideas with two or three classmates. Once you have finished brainstorming, use the space below to write your group's Text Reformulation. Each group member should write down the reformulation. Continue your reformulation on the back of this sheet if necessary.

....

....

....

....

....

....

....

....

....

....

....

....

....

....

Part 2. Directions: Based on your reading and Text Reformulation of the excerpt from *Volcano*, answer the following questions on the lines provided.

1. What was the cause of the avalanche on Mount St. Helens?

Effect: The avalanche

Cause: ....

2. What was the cause of the leveling of the forests around Mount St. Helens?

Effect: The leveling of the forests around Mount St. Helens

Cause: ....

3. What was the effect of the ash, rock, and pumice settling on the melting snow?

Cause: Ash, rock, and pumice settling on the melting snow

Effect: ....

The Dog of Pompeii / *from* Volcano

SKILL COMPARING AND CONTRASTING TEXTS | **STRATEGY** LIKERT SCALES

Part 1. Directions: After reading "The Dog of Pompeii" (Pupil's Edition, page 513) and "Volcano" (Pupil's Edition, page 498), respond to each of the following items by marking the letter *V* in the circle you choose for "Volcano" and the letter *D* in the circle you choose for "The Dog of Pompeii." Then, explain your choices on the lines provided.

1. This selection was interesting to read.

    ◯   ◯   ◯   ◯
STRONGLY AGREE   **AGREE**   **DISAGREE**   **STRONGLY DISAGREE**

Explanation: ....

2. This selection presented information about how volcanoes are formed.

    ◯   ◯   ◯   ◯
STRONGLY AGREE   **AGREE**   **DISAGREE**   **STRONGLY DISAGREE**

Explanation: ....

3. This selection helped me feel what it's like to be near an erupting volcano.

    ◯   ◯   ◯   ◯
STRONGLY AGREE   **AGREE**   **DISAGREE**   **STRONGLY DISAGREE**

Explanation: ....

4. This selection would be helpful in providing facts for a research paper.

    ◯   ◯   ◯   ◯
STRONGLY AGREE   **AGREE**   **DISAGREE**   **STRONGLY DISAGREE**

Explanation: ....

5. This selection could be the basis for a good movie script.

    ◯   ◯   ◯   ◯
STRONGLY AGREE   **AGREE**   **DISAGREE**   **STRONGLY DISAGREE**

Explanation: ....

Part 2. Directions: After reading "The Dog of Pompeii" and "Volcano," use your own paper to complete a Venn diagram like the one below. Fill in the circles with comparisons and contrasts between the two selections. Consider the kind of text each selection represents (historical narrative and informative writing), the events in each selection, and the use of certain details and elements, such as characters, terms, language, graphic aids, and description.

The Dog of Pompeii   Both   Volcano

Why the Bat Flies at Night

1   You might think that bats have always slept through the day and hunted for food through the night. That's not true! At least it's not true if you believe the legend of the Zapotec people of Mexico.

2   Long, long ago, soon after God finished making the world, the Bat lived like the birds. He built his nest in trees and ate seeds like the other birds. The Bat was a good neighbor to the birds, too. He did not bother the Cardinal's babies as they napped in their nests in the tall pines. He stepped aside when the Crow swooped down to the river to refresh herself in the water.

3   One day as the Bat sat by a pond, he saw his reflection in the still water. He jumped back in fright. "I'm so ugly!" the Bat said. "Look at me! I don't look anything like a bird!

4   "Instead of a beautiful crest like the Jay, I wear a cap of short fur on my head. I don't have a beak like the Parrot. I have a squished pug nose and lips and teeth. No bird has teeth! Plus, my body is furry, and my wings look like brown leather. I'm not dressed in a beautiful cloak of feathers like the Macaw. I'm ugly, ugly, ugly!"

5   The Bat was very depressed until he had an idea. "Maybe God will help me change how I look," he thought.

6   The Bat was clever. He knew that God would refuse to change his appearance just because he looked different from other flying creatures. God wanted all his creations to be different. The Bat needed to give God a better reason to make him beautiful.

7   The Bat decided he would trick God into granting his wish. All it would take was one very harmless lie: He would tell God he got too cold when he flew.

8   "If I really consider it," thought the Bat, "the lie is almost the truth. I do get a little chilly when I fly up high. Doesn't that grain of truth make my lie so small and harmless, even God won't guess I'm tricking him?" He muttered to himself,

9   "I get cold when I fly,

10   That's a small, harmless lie."

11   The Bat stayed so busy repeating this rhyme that he didn't realize the Crow had overheard him.

12   The Bat began the long journey to God's kingdom. He flew for many days and nights, over one thousand mountains. All the while he repeated the rhyme to himself. By the time the Bat reached God's kingdom, he almost believed the small, harmless lie.

13   "I honor you, Great One," the Bat said, bowing before God. "I've flown for many days and nights, over one hundred canyons, past five hundred rivers, and above one thousand mountains to ask you to grant me a favor."

14   God nodded, inviting the Bat to continue.

15   "No one can say your creations are not perfect, Great One, and I least of all," the Bat said. "I am just a humble, ugly bat. You also kindly gave me leathery wings so I can fly and soft fur to keep me warm as I glide through the sky."

16   The Bat paused to catch his breath. He almost lost his nerve. Could he really trick God? Then the Bat thought,

17   "I get cold when I fly,

18   That's a small, harmless lie."

I've got nothing to lose, the Bat decided.

19   "However, there is a problem, my Master. I get terribly cold when I fly," the Bat said.

20   "What of that? Why don't you fly less often?" said God.

21   "It is my place to fly," said the Bat. "In that way I am a bird. Don't you think I could stay warm if you dressed me in feathers like the birds?" The Bat made a great show of shivering and chattering his teeth as if he were cold.

22   God felt sorry for the small, unhappy-looking creature before him.

23   "It is too late to give you feathers. I've given all the feathers to the birds. I will order the birds to give one feather each to you. That way you'll be warm when you fly," said God.

24   In no time the birds followed God's bidding, each giving one feather to the Bat. Soon the Bat looked simply wonderful! If you had seen him, you would have been amazed at his

white feather from the Sea Gull's belly, his blue feather from the Jay's shoulder, his red feather from the Robin's breast, his purple feather from the Painted Bunting's brow, his yellow feather from the Goldfinch's chin, his black feather from the  Raven's wing, his striped, rusty brown feather from the Turkey's tail, and the bright green feather given, with great fuss, by the Parrot.

25   Even the Parrot had to admit the Bat looked pretty good. The Bat was overjoyed. When he flew in a great arc high above the heads of the Zapotec people, they saw the rainbow for the first time.

26   The Bat grew vain with all the attention he received. He began to snub his neighbor birds. Just to show off, he buzzed the pines where the Cardinal kept her nest, frightening the babies. He spent hours strutting along the riverside, looking at his reflection in the water. He chased off any bird who dared disturb his reflection by taking a drink.

27   The Crow observed this behavior from her treetop nest and decided to call a group of the birds together. All the birds flew over one hundred canyons, past five hundred rivers, and above one thousand mountains to ask God to punish the Bat. In a great roaring ruckus, they squawked and whistled to God their protests against the Bat. The Parrot complained loudest and longest. "I'm cold because of losing my feather." Only the Crow stayed quiet as all the other birds whined. Finally, God silenced them all. The Crow stepped forward.

28   "Great One, you are kind. We all honor you," she said. "However, I heard the Bat say something you should know. I

think the Bat tricked you with a lie."

29   "What!" bellowed God. "The Bat tricked me? What did the Bat say?"

30   "He said . . .", The Crow cleared her throat. Then, she recited.

31   "I get cold when I fly,

32   That's a small, harmless lie."

33   "So I was tricked!" the Mighty One roared. "I will teach the Bat a lesson he will not soon forget."

34   God was so angry that he whisked the birds back to their homes in a flash. Then, God decided how to teach the Bat a lesson.

35   The next day as the Bat was flying above the heads of the Zapotec people, every feather began to drop away from his body.

36   The Bat landed on the ground in shock. He had gotten used to the warm feather cloak, and without it, he really *was* cold. The chill was nothing, though, compared to the cold fear the Bat felt when he heard God's voice speaking to him.

37   "To suit yourself, you tricked me. You lied so I would make you more beautiful than all the birds. I will punish you and every bat that comes after you for these deeds," said God.

38   "After tonight, you will no longer be out with my other creatures," God said. "You, who spent so much time admiring yourself, will only be able to sense the way you look. You tricked me with a lie and said you were cold when you fly. Well, you will be cold now. When you fly, you will no longer have the sun to warm you. You will fly only at night and feel the cold night breezes grabbing at your wings. You will live in damp, dark caves. Never again will you have a cozy nest in the trees. You will search and search for the feathers you lost, but you will never find them. This I command."

39   Thus, to this day, bats fly only at night. They come out at dusk from their caves and fly against the moon in a strange, looping flight, the Zapotec legend says, always looking for their feathers as if they were blind.

Mini Read

Why the Bat Flies at Night

SKILL ESTABLISHING PURPOSES FOR READING | **STRATEGY** PROBABLE PASSAGE

Part 1. Directions: Before reading the MiniRead "Why the Bat Flies at Night," study the following words and phrases and then place them in the appropriate categories. Next, complete the Probable Passage by filling in the blanks. Some words may be used more than once.

Words and Phrases from "Why the Bat Flies at Night" to Sort:

soon after God made the world ugly deceiving God
gets cold when flying the Crow given many feathers
fly at night and live in caves God punishment
looking for his lost feathers vain the Bat

Categories for Sorting Words and Phrases:

Setting	
Characters	
Problem(s)	
Solution(s)	
Ending	

Probable Passage to Complete:

The story takes place [1] _____. The main characters are [2] _____,

[3] _____, and [4] _____. The problem is that the Bat feels he is

[5] _____. The Bat deals with this problem by [6] _____. He does this by saying he

[7] _____. The Bat is then [8] _____. However, he becomes [9] _____, and

he is inconsiderate of the other birds, so [10] _____ tells [11] _____ that the Bat has

lied. God decides that the Bat's [12] _____ will be to [13] _____, forever

[14] _____.

Part 2. Directions: Before reading the MiniRead, answer the following questions on the lines provided.

1. What type of selection do you predict this will be?

....

....

2. Based on your prediction, which of these purposes for reading would you establish? (gaining information, solving a problem, making a discovery, interpreting an event, being entertained)

....

The Seventh Sister

SKILL ESTABLISHING PURPOSES FOR READING | **STRATEGY** PROBABLE PASSAGE

Part 1. Directions: Before reading "The Seventh Sister" (Pupil's Edition, page 528), study the following words and phrases and then place them in the appropriate categories. Next, complete the Probable Passage by filling in the blanks. You may use a word or phrase more than once.

Words and Phrases from "The Seventh Sister" to Sort:

return home   Chang   grassy lowlands of China

stay together   neglecting her work   the heavens above

Mei   sad and lonely

Categories for Sorting Words and Phrases:

Settings	Character(s)	Problem(s)	Solution(s)

Probable Passage to Complete:

The story takes place in the [1] _____ and [2] _____. The main characters are
[3] _____ and [4] _____. One of the problems is that the two main characters feel
[5] _____. Chang takes care of this problem by stealing [6] _____'s gown, without
which she cannot return to [7] _____. The two fall in love and [8] _____. However,
another problem comes up because Mei is [9] _____, which is to weave the tapestry of the
night sky. The couple agree that she must [10] _____, which makes them both very sad.

Part 2. Directions: Before reading "The Seventh Sister," answer the following questions on the lines provided.

1. What type of selection do you predict this will be?

   ....

   ....

2. Based on your prediction, which of these purposes for reading would you establish? (gaining information, solving a problem, making a discovery, interpreting an event, being entertained)

   ....

   ....

ELEMENTS OF LITERATURE

Scanning the Heavens

Part 1. Directions: Decide with a partner whether you will read "Scanning the Heavens" (Pupil's Edition, page 538) silently or aloud. As you read, stop every two or three paragraphs and take turns saying something about what you just read, including any comments you can make about establishing purposes for reading. In the chart below, write a check mark in the appropriate column for each type of comment you make.

Prediction	Comment	Question	Connection

Part 2. Directions: Think about the Say Something dialogue you had with your partner, and answer the following questions on the lines provided.

1. If someone had been listening in on your Say Something dialogue, what would he or she have heard? Give a summary.

2. Did you answer any questions for your partner? Did your partner answer any questions for you? If so, what were your questions? What questions remain unanswered?

3. According to the Say Something chart above, what type of comment did you make the most? Why do you think you made that type of comment the most?

4. What would you say was your purpose for reading this selection, and why?

Medusa's Head

SKILL COMPARING STORY VARIANTS | **STRATEGY** TEXT REFORMULATION

Part 1. Directions: After you have read "Medusa's Head" (Pupil's Edition, page 572), form a small group and brainstorm about what type of reformulation you want to use for the selection: a journal entry or a *Fortunately/Unfortunately* pattern. Then, work individually to create the reformulation. Use the space below and the back of this page if necessary to write your reformulation.

....

....

....

....

....

....

....

....

....

....

....

....

Part 2. Directions: After writing your reformulation, answer the following questions on the lines provided.

1. What kinds of information did you leave out of your reformulation?

....

....

2. What kinds of information did you include in your reformulation?

....

....

3. What are the biggest differences between your reformulation and the original "Medusa's Head"?

....

....

Welcome Your Guests with Hospitality

1 "If I knew you were coming, I'd have baked a cake." So went a popular song in the 1950s. When you know friends or relatives are coming over, you usually try to prepare for their visit because you want them to feel welcome. Whether it's a Thanksgiving dinner your family has been planning for weeks or just a friend dropping by with a new video game, food and drinks are usually part of your welcome. You are showing your hospitality.

2 All over the world people practice hospitality. They take extra steps to make sure guests are comfortable and happy. In a fast trip around the world, you would find many differences in food, drink, and customs regarding hospitality.

3 For a special experience, visit Mexico on November 2, the Day of the Dead. In many homes, people will be honoring and remembering their dead loved ones. It is more a celebration than a time of sadness.

4 Your Mexican hosts take garden tools, flowers, and candles to the graveyard. There, you help them pull weeds, clean the area, and decorate the grave and headstone. You then share a picnic with tasty foods. Tamales, tubes of corn meal packed around finely chopped meat, are the main dish. Stuffed chiles, beans, and rice flavored with tomatoes are also enjoyed.

5 The star of the picnic is a bread Mexicans eat only on the Day of the Dead. *Pan de muertos* is sweet white bread made to look like skulls, bones, or coffins. Toy decorations or toppings of bright pink sugar make pan de muertos more fun than creepy.

pan de muertos
(pän dā mŏŏ er´ tōs)

6 Next, travel to the city of Tangier, where your Moroccan hosts want to show you how generous they are. They offer more food and drinks than you can eat because they want you to leave their house fully satisfied.

ELEMENTS OF LITERATURE

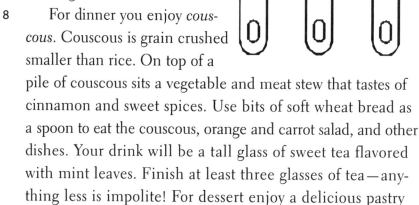

7   Your hosts eat at low, round tables. Before and after a meal, a pan of water, soap, and a small towel are passed around for hand washing. Why is that? While some Moroccans use spoons, forks, and plates to eat, most eat in the traditional way. Everyone scoops up food with their hands from big bowls and platters. Polite Moroccans use their right hands to eat.

couscous
(kōōs´ kōōs)

8   For dinner you enjoy *couscous*. Couscous is grain crushed smaller than rice. On top of a pile of couscous sits a vegetable and meat stew that tastes of cinnamon and sweet spices. Use bits of soft wheat bread as a spoon to eat the couscous, orange and carrot salad, and other dishes. Your drink will be a tall glass of sweet tea flavored with mint leaves. Finish at least three glasses of tea—anything less is impolite! For dessert enjoy a delicious pastry stuffed with almonds.

9   Your next stop is Hue, a city in Vietnam, a long, narrow country on the South China Sea in Southeast Asia. Your hosts provide you with a different meal.

10   Whether it is breakfast, lunch, or dinner, Vietnamese hosts offer you a beef noodle soup called Pho Bo. Even though much of Vietnam is tropical in climate, people there eat hot soup at most meals. You eat the noodles with chopsticks and slurp the broth straight from the bowl.

11   You also use chopsticks to eat a spicy dinner of vegetables fried with chicken, fish, or beef. Try some meat cooked with fruit and served with rice. Have a "packet" salad of shrimp, rice noodles, and cucumber rolled up in lettuce leaves. Just pop the little packets into your mouth the way your Vietnamese hosts do.

NOTES

12   Expect to have fruit for dessert. Lucky guests get *litchi*, a husked fruit that looks like a white grape. It reveals a big brown seed when you peel it. Peeled litchis look like eyeballs, but they taste so good, you eat many.

13   Finally, pay a visit to Sweden. Located in northern Europe, Sweden has snowy winters that last as many as ten months. Because the winters are so long, the Swedes try extra hard to have parties full of good cheer, and they like to show their generosity.

14   While in Sweden, enjoy a *smorgasbord* dinner. This Swedish word means "bread and butter table." Generous Swedish hosts prepare at least six smorgasbord dishes and as many as sixty foods! Hosts arrange platters of food on a buffet table. Guests line up and serve themselves small helpings of food on their own plates. Every smorgasbord includes a fish called herring. You eat the fish first and then feast on pickles, boiled potatoes, and hot or cold salads. Then your hosts serve hot dishes such as omelets, filled pancakes, and meatballs in gravy. For dessert, taste several cheeses and crunchy rye bread.

15   No matter where in the world you go, people practice hospitality. How does your family practice it? What special things do *you* do to welcome your guests?

litchi
(lē´ chē)

smorgasbord
(smôr´ gəs bôrd)

ELEMENTS OF LITERATURE

Mini Read

Welcome Your Guests with Hospitality

SKILL RECOGNIZING THEMES THAT CROSS CULTURES | **STRATEGY** LIKERT SCALES

Part 1. Directions: After reading the MiniRead "Welcome Your Guests with Hospitality," respond to each of the following scales by circling whether you *Strongly Agree, Agree, Disagree,* or *Strongly Disagree* with each statement. Be sure to support your choices with examples from the MiniRead.

1. Hospitality is a worldwide practice.

Strongly Agree | (Agree) | Disagree | Strongly Disagree

Explanation: So you can learn hospitality.

2. All the cultures mentioned in the MiniRead show hospitality differently.

(Strongly Agree) | Agree | Disagree | Strongly Disagree

Explanation: Some hospitality are differrent.

3. According to this MiniRead, being a good host means providing a good meal for your guests.

(Strongly Agree) | Agree | Disagree | Strongly Disagree

Explanation: They will do the same thing to you.

4. Hospitality is more gratifying for the guests than for the hosts.

Strongly Agree | Agree | (Disagree) | Strongly Disagree

Explanation: It could be for both.

5. This MiniRead includes information about why each culture practices hospitality.

Strongly Agree | (Agree) | Disagree | Strongly Disagree

Explanation: It could help you.

6. This MiniRead explains the most important aspects of hospitality.

Strongly Agree | (Agree) | Disagree | Strongly Disagree

Explanation: So you wont mess up

Part 2. Directions: On the lines provided, answer the following question.

7. How did completing the Likert Scales above help you to recognize connections that cross cultures in the MiniRead? because it helped.

ELEMENTS OF LITERATURE

Baucis and Philemon

SKILL RECOGNIZING THEMES THAT CROSS CULTURES | **STRATEGY** LIKERT SCALES

Part 1. Directions: After reading "Baucis and Philemon" (Pupil's Edition, page 589), respond to each of the following scales by circling whether you *Strongly Agree, Agree, Disagree,* or *Strongly Disagree* with each statement. Be sure to support your choices with examples from the selection.

1. Baucis and Philemon demonstrate the most important aspects of hospitality.

| Strongly Agree | Agree | Disagree | Strongly Disagree |

Explanation: *They gave their food away for a week*

2. It isn't fair for all travelers to expect hospitality from every host.

| Strongly Agree | Agree | Disagree | Strongly Disagree |

Explanation: *I may need the food or steel*

3. Baucis and Philemon deserved their reward for their hospitality.

| Strongly Agree | Agree | Disagree | Strongly Disagree |

Explanation: *They deserved it because they never asked qustions.*

4. There are many similarities between ancient Greek hospitality and hospitality in the United States today.

| Strongly Agree | Agree | Disagree | Strongly Disagree |

Explanation: *Some people are kind.*

5. This kind of hospitality should still be practiced today, even though our way of life is very different from that of the ancient Greeks.

| Strongly Agree | Agree | Disagree | Strongly Disagree |

Explanation:

Part 2. Directions: Answer the following questions on the lines provided. Continue your answers on the back of this sheet if necessary.

6. What is the theme of "Baucis and Philemon"? *Be kind to others*

7. How does this theme show itself in U.S. culture? *9-11-01*

Quetzalcoatl

Part 1. Directions: Before reading "Quetzalcoatl" (Pupil's Edition, page 599), read the following words and phrases, and then sort them into the categories that appear in the chart below. Then, use the same words and phrases to complete the Probable Passage. Save Part 2 until you've read the story "Quetzalcoatl."

Words and Phrases to Sort:

the neighbors envy the Toltecs' prosperity   go back to his homeland
Tezcatlipoca   welcome Cortés as their returning god
gets the king-god drunk   Quetzalcoatl
southern Mexico

Categories for Sorting Words and Phrases:

Setting	
Character(s)	
Problem(s)	
Solution(s)	
Ending	

Probable Passage to Complete:

The story mainly takes place in [1] _____. The main characters are [2] _____, king-god of the Toltecs, and [3] _____, chief of the neighbors' gods. The problem is that [4] _____, so Tezcatlipoca [5] _____ and ruins the Toltecs. When Quetzalcoatl sees what has happened, his only solution is to [6] _____ in despair. The people wait many years for his return, and, in the end, they [7] _____.

Part 2. Directions: After you've read "Quetzalcoatl," complete the following statement.
My Probable Passage differed from "Quetzalcoatl" in these ways:

....

....

....

Ali Baba and the Forty Thieves

SKILL USING WORD PARTS | **STRATEGY** VOCABULARY DEVELOPMENT: VOCABULARY TREES

Directions: The story "Ali Baba and the Forty Thieves" (Pupil's Edition, page 610) has many words that you can break down into word parts. In the first three pages of the story, there are eight words that contain the suffix –ly, which means "in a certain way." You can learn to figure out words that use the common suffix –ly by creating a vocabulary tree. To make your vocabulary tree:

1. Write the suffix –ly in the root area of the tree. Then, write the meaning of –ly, "in a certain way," next to it.

2. Reread pages 611–613 of the story. Look for seven words that have the –ly suffix as a word part. Write the first –ly word you find in the trunk of the tree. Then, every time you come across a new –ly word in the story, write it in one of the branches until all the branches contain an –ly word.

3. Based on the suffix meaning, try to figure out the meaning of each word. Write a definition next to the word in the branch. Use a dictionary to check your work.

4. In the twigs of each branch, describe where you have read, heard, or used the word before. One example has been completed for you.

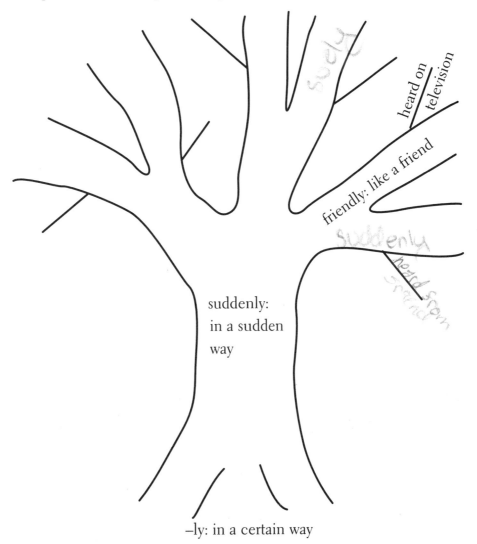

ELEMENTS OF LITERATURE

ADDITIONAL PRACTICE

Strategy: It Says ... I Say

Question	It Says ... (What the text says)	I Say ... (My thoughts)	And So ... (My inference)

Strategy: It Says ... I Say

Question	It Says ... (What the text says)	I Say ... (My thoughts)	And So ... (My inference)

Strategy: It Says . . . I Say

Question	It Says . . . (What the text says)	I Say . . . (My thoughts)	And So . . . (My inference)

Strategy: Say Something

In the chart below, write a check mark in the appropriate column for each type of "Say Something" comment you make.

Prediction	Comment	Question	Connection

Think about the Say Something dialogue you had with your partner, and answer the following questions on the lines provided.

1. If someone had been listening in on your Say Something dialogue, what would they have heard? Give a summary. ....

....

2. Did you answer any questions for your partner? Did your partner answer any questions for you? What were the questions? What questions remain unanswered? ....

....

3. Looking at your chart above, what type of comment did you make the most? Why do you think you made that type the most? ....

....

4. If you do a Say Something again, how will you do it differently? ....

....

....

Strategy: Say Something

In the chart below, write a check mark in the appropriate column for each type of "Say Something" comment you make.

Prediction	Comment	Question	Connection

Think about the Say Something dialogue you had with your partner, and answer the following questions on the lines provided.

1. If someone had been listening in on your Say Something dialogue, what would they have heard? Give a summary. ....

....

2. Did you answer any questions for your partner? Did your partner answer any questions for you? What were the questions? What questions remain unanswered? ....

....

3. Looking at your chart above, what type of comment did you make the most? Why do you think you made that type the most? ....

....

4. If you do a Say Something again, how will you do it differently? ....

....

....

Strategy: Somebody Wanted But So

Somebody	Wanted	But	So

     ELEMENTS OF LITERATURE

Strategy: Somebody Wanted But So

Somebody	Wanted	But	So

Strategy: Somebody Wanted But So

Somebody	Wanted	But	So

Strategy: Think-Aloud

Think-Aloud Tally Sheet

Listener:_____

Think-Aloud Comments	Tally
Making predictions	
Picturing the text	
Making comparisons	
Identifying problems	
Fixing problems	
Making a comment	

Strategy: Think-Aloud

Think-Aloud Tally Sheet   Listener:_____

Think-Aloud Comments	Tally
Making predictions	
Picturing the text	
Making comparisons	
Identifying problems	
Fixing problems	
Making a comment	